TRANSFORMATION IN BANKING:

BY

COMPLIANCE, IDENTINOMICS & DIGITALISATION

By Chaturbhuja Barik

चरन्मार्गान्वजिानाति

A wanderer (eventually) finds the path.

PREFACE

In the *Mahabharata*, **Dhritarashtra** was crowned King of **Hastinapur** at the time of the **Kurukshetra War**, the epic's climactic event. Dhritarashtra was blind from birth fathered one hundred sons (and one **daughter**) who came to be known as the **Kauravas**. **Duryodhana**, his eldest son, led the Kauravas to the war.

Before the war precipitated, Lord **Krishna** travelled to Hastinapur as a peace emissary of Pandavas trying to persuade Kauravas, to prevent the bloodshed of their kin. However, Duryodhana not only rejected and ignored his plea but conspired to arrest him. Thus, Krishna's peace mission failed and led to war. Maharshi **Vyasa** offered a divine vision to Dhritarashtra, so that Dhritarashtra could see the war, since he was unable to go to the battlefield. Dhritarashtra asked that the boon to be given to Sanjay, the charioteer, not willing to see his kin slaughtered. But when Lord Krishna displayed his Vishvarupa (Universal Form) to **Arjuna** on the battlefield of **Kurukshetra**, Dhritarashtra regretted not possessing the divine sight. Sanjaya narrated the war, reporting how **Bhima** killed all his children and consoled the blind king and challenged the king with his viewpoints and morals.

4

He was confident that Bhishma, **Drona**, **Karna**, and other invincible warriors would make the Kauravas victorious. Dhritrashtra rejoiced whenever the tide of war turned against Pandavas. However, the results of the war-devastated him. He saw all his trueborn sons died in the carnage. Dhritarashtra's only daughter Duhsala was widowed. The only son of Dhritrashtra who survived the Kurukshetra War was Yuyutsu, since he had defected to the Pandavas side at the onset of war.

MANAGEMENT SUTRA:

The grand epic of The Mahabharata is an encyclopedia that shows us beyond good and evil and the path that needs to be taken before, during, and after the crisis.

Dhritarashtra not only failed to accept the offer of The Lord Krishna but missed the opportunity of getting divine vision offered to feel the happenings in the war of Kurukshetra. He could have provided a scope of mid-way correction opportunity, had he seen the war himself, which could have saved the battle. But a blind belief on the stalwarts of his kingdom, undermining Lord Krishna's masterplan, was a very regressive step taken by the blind king.

The cut-throat competition of the financial market is akin to the war of Kurukshetra. All players are fighting hard and vying and capturing a larger share of the market pie. Some of the players have brought in disruptive changes in the business landscape through technology, innovation, and aggressive customer service. These changes are inevitable and need to be accommodated and aligned with before they take a toll.

RBI, MOF, Policy Makers, and Top Management are trying to reconcile for a better adaptation of the process and the way one must accept these changes, much like Lord Krishna. By failing to adopt and adhere to these changes, we are undermining the role of Lord Krishna, who has definite plans, and we are refusing the offers from Lord Krishna to change. Do we believe our strongholds like CASA, branch network, and a great legacy like Dhritarashtra blindly?

We, the members of BANKS, need to ponder and ensure that we do not end up like Dhritarashtra, for failing to heed to these changes. Also, we must not leave the divine vision only for Sanjay to listen and interpret the whole episode.

For, if the answer is 'YES,' then Dhritarashtra must face the humiliation of losing the battle and even failure to witness the great learning from Viswarup.

LESSONS: The only painful and unforgiving statement that we, as a banker, would ever listen is ….

THUS, SPAKE DHRITARASHTRA IF I WERE NOT BLIND………

> I see technology as a means to
> empower and as a tool that
> bridges the distance between
> hope and opportunity.
> Social media is reducing social
> barriers. It connects people on
> the strength of human values,
> not identities.

> Narendra Modi

7

CHAPTER 1: NEED FOR TRANSFORMATION

If you think compliance is
expensive, try non-compliance.

Paul Macnulty

Introduction

The basic rule that we learned from our childhood about taking the left side of the road always reminds us how the change is constant. Now with the improvement of infrastructure of two-lane, four-lane and multi-lane roads, the basic rule that we learned has changed over a while. Now you can take the right side of the way too.

So, transformation in policy, process, and attitude is required in everyday life. Moreover, in the financial sector, the digitalization effect created an atmosphere where continuous innovation is the key to sustain. The rules are changing in a super speed. Look at emerging technologies like Artificial Intelligence, Robotics, big data analytics, the Internet of things, etc., every development in these fields poses a threat to the process we use in the financial sector and eventually the product offered. The changes are becoming more transforming in nature day by day due to rising influence of regulations, digital competition in financial services, more innovative players in micro-segment, ever-demanding customer expectations, and finally, the developments around the world. In our country, the Unified Payment Interface (UPI) created a revolution like an open banking system that needs to be addressed by individual

9

banks to take advantage of others in terms of data and customer retention. The UPI system simply allows a customer to choose any Digital platform she likes irrespective of his base banker. It means if a person has an account in bank A, she is not compelled to use the platform provided by bank A to accesses her accounts; in turn, she can opt any other bank or even fintech companies.

Worldwide talk about open banking platforms is relevant to us like regulations as PSD2 in the European Union and similar rules in other parts of the world. Once this open banking comes into force, the way we do banking is going to change and specifically for PSBs in India. The percentage of total business might reduce due to these types of changes happening in the market, which is seen as the Pulverization of banking business, pulverization financial technology platform. Besides these, the dependence of customers on technology is waving towards branchless banking fueled by demonetization and steps towards a less-cash economy. We are moving towards a phase where few people will visit our bank branches, denouncing our style of marketing and functioning, and the pace is too fast to catch hold. The expectations of customers increase along with the speed of

Digitalization and innovation.so to have a more fabulous customer experience, continuous innovation is required.

Digitalization related transformation brings cyber risk and risks associated with operational knowledge and cultural differences, which is the most significant threat of the century. Hence compliance of the security norms and cyber insurance becomes a priority. The current trend of banking is moving towards the rising NPAs as well as policy reforms. Hence the challenges arising thereby need to be addressed by using compliance, technology, and transformation in processes and people.

To summarize, Digitalization, continuous disruptive innovation, regulatory strictness, global economic environment, macroeconomic environment of our country, change in Govt policies demanded more focus on the way we function and its transformation. And the transformation is to be in such a way that it is secured, fulfilling expectations of consumers and with an opportunity of continuous innovation meeting future need arising from the banking sector and the world as a whole.

So, we need to look beyond our boundaries and look for alternatives. Let us focus upon specific movements in the market socially economically and structurally, which will change the way we think about our banks.

That which does not kill us makes us

stronger.

Friedrich Nietzsche

A creative man is motivated

by the desire to achieve, not by the

desire to beat others.   Ayn Rand

TRUST

Out of the several challenges we face in the financial sector, "TRUST" is the fundamental one to care. Meanwhile, the financial crisis of 2008, a substantial question has been how banks can restore the trust of their clients. Research has demonstrated that perceived trustworthiness includes three elements: ability (are you competent?), integrity (are you honest?), and benevolence (do you care about my interests?). Both competence and integrity are recurring themes in many discussions concerning the financial crisis. Kindness, however, is not used very often – if at all. At the same time, banking clients mainly express concerns about whether the Bank cares about their interests as well as their interests. Put simply, a particular "morality of care" is missing in the discussion.

As a consequence, it also seems to be missing from efforts to restore trust in banks. Only trust will be built when clients perceive that benevolence, truly felt, is underlying the decisions and actions of their Bank. Banks must be able to connect with their clients on a personal level. Unfortunately, banks are increasingly investing in the efficient use of IT applications, and as a consequence, are removing the individual element necessary for

13

true benevolent interactions with clients. And until the board and top management model, the value of benevolence – as something to demonstrate, not just talk about – levels of trust will remain low.

The significant survival recipe of PSUs is the trust that was built up for decades. With private banks at the beginning of this millennium, it was lacking, and continuously, they build up this trust. We expect the same from payment banks and wallet players. And as the new generation is taking over the customer base of ours, winning their trust is much more critical. So we must work efficiently to make our customer base robust and loyal.

Later, we will discuss about the toolbox for transformation where we will emphasize on restoring and enhancing trust by Digitalization, compliance, and IDENTINOMICS.

The future influences the present just as much as the past.

Friedrich Nietzsche

Technology shift

Customer expectations are changing in line with evolving technological experiences. With the advent of a new technological breakthrough like Cloud computing, Artificial Intelligence (AI), robotics, IoT, blockchain, and biometrics fueled by demonetization and less cash economy now, the situation is like waging war with technology. We must focus on upgrading ourselves fine-tuning with modern technology. Also, we must provide the services at par with peers in the fields like Apps banking and E-banking with technological empathy.

Cloud computing is a technology that is used to store software and data, and it doesn't require any computer service at owners company. Blockchain allows to design distributed software such as the Bitcoin. Robotics takes over many labour-intensive tasks in the financial sector. Biometrics provides new means to authenticate, for instance of paying, through its fingerprints. IoT provides scope for linking all the objects and processes with each other via the internet to overcome hurdles in communication, monitoring, and compliance. And finally, artificial intelligence, describes computer or software that can know what you need before you know.

After the advent of the digital age, the fastest change that is happening anywhere in the digital sphere. Digital technology provides the scope for numerous innovations in any field of operation. Again, as these changes are new to the world, the changes are swift and evasive. The financial sector is not far from the effects of this change. Digital technology pulverized the whole gamut of the business segment. For example, a change in the way we provide passbook changes without changing the entire structure of banking operation. Or any innovation related to payment is always subjected to disruption. As the scope of digital innovation is unlimited and continuous, new technologies mentioned above are influencing the way we do banking.

For example, the most talked-about of this field is Blockchain technology, as this technology gains popularity among banking communities, acceptability of this will increase too. The implementation will result in much faster and safer banking, so all the banks that are using the traditional technology must adopt this disruptive technology. It is disruptive because this will be available more cheaply and popularly to the common mass. So the fundamental threat to the banking system is the fastness of change in the technology sphere. So to be in the market evolution and adoption of the banking system is an essential feature. We are looking at the past when we have moved from manual mode to banking dependent on computers, again from computers to core banking, which took more than decades to shift from one another. But now the adoption is changing very fast using the latest developments.

Also, we have to consider the cost of technology up-gradation and return from this investment. The return must be amortized in a short period, unlike before. The impact of this on cost will affect the increase in prices of the products and services we offer, again, which will create a market where the scale and cost-efficient methods will count. This will pose a challenge to reimagining business strategies adopted in the banks.

The only wrong move when it comes to digital transformation is not to make any move at all - Didier Bonnet, Senior VP Capgemini

Demography shift

Most of our loyal customers are either retiring or leaving the business, and the gen-next customers are occupying more percentage. This necessitates our products and procedures to be according to their need and compatibility. Changes in generation, change agility, technology adaptability, and loyalty. This particular period can be seen as a mixture of NextGen customers (Digital Natives) and old generation customers (Digital Immigrants). Digital natives are those groups of persons who are born with the digital revolution and their counterpart called digital immigrants who learned digital for their requirement.

The new customers in the market today belong to the native digital category. This generation is currently the most significant demographic cohort in the world. They are typically highly educated and are tech-savvy. And, they have grown up in a world with social media and mobile technologies. They can't imagine a different world. As customers, these groups insisting on convenience are focused on innovation, lacking brand loyalty and always connected. Now the critical question is, how do we attract this Generation? We get them through smartphones. These groups

18

of consumers are not just mobile-first consumers. They're mobile-only; they are always linked to the mobile equipments. They are expected to be able to use them efficiently and securely to interact with the world. This generation is also multi-tasking, they suppose to take care of the banking needs, while they wait for a bus. Reserving one day, a month for banking is simply not tolerable. This means that they want to have information and do their financial business in snack size. They also wish to all interactions to be personalized, contextualized, and as fast as possible. They have no interest and tolerance for reading a catalogue. All they want to know and expect to get to know from banks is if they can buy that thing. And if they do, what else do they have to sacrifice. They know what the latest technology can do, and they are likely to be aware of innovative features, through the social channels. So, what is happening when we provide offerings to the mobile, personalized, creative, and comes in snack size. These customers are likely to have several financial arrangements going on at the same time. And gradually, they slide towards the most favourable pull. And that is how companies bring them over by providing services that ticks all these boxes. Banks earn the right to do more and more business with this Generation. But for many incumbents, the question is reversed. What will happen if banks don't provide this? Frankly, customers will move elsewhere. They were not satisfied with what banks can offer, until they have an excellent reason not to stay.

To sum up, banks need to change as per the requirement of digital natives. So considerable investments in digital technology, digital empathy, trust, and all mobile banks need to be established. That requires a substantial transformation in the technology sphere, attitude of employees, and change in marketing style. This will help us to capture the next generation of businesses and individuals into our fold when the older generation retires.

Social media has created a historical shift from the historically powerful to the historically powerless. Now everyone has a voice ~ Sheryl Sandberg, COO, Facebook

---

Knowledge shift

Essential skill requirements for performing duties in banks are transformed a lot in the coming days. If we can travel back and find accounting and credit dispensation was the most required skillset that comprised of adding a considerable number of balances or likewise jobs. But with computerization and use of calculator, made that skill redundant. As of now, those works are performed by computer algorithms. So as the case of credit dispensation, the use of modern processes and data availability reshaped the way we financed retail, MSME, and agriculture. Loan automation processes reduced both risk and time taken for credit. Similarly, most of the methods that we have adopted in the past become redundant and new processes fueled by technology taken the driver's seat.

Those factors, too, created a need and vacuum in the industry; unique skill sets are required to deal with changes in this sector. Like, cybersecurity professionals, law professionals with Information technology, risk managers, big data analysts, software programmers are much sought professions than that of what we have now in our offices. For example, data analysts are required to extract data, collect and analyses them for banks to manage risks, credit modelling, credit dispensation, and marketing of products.

So the question arises, do we have these professionals and can acquire quality people in this regard and build a structure to absorb future business expectations. This is one of the real challenges that our system is going to face. When the wisdom of every new field is not accumulated for further progress, we need people of exceptional ability to do the same. For this, we must recruit potential candidates or start training our potential inhouse candidates to build the wisdom. Hence the immediate need is to segregate the areas where we are facing knowledge shift and begin building a structure and people to meet the challenges. The significant regions might be in the field of cybersecurity, business analytics, big data analytics, risk managers. So, for future stability in the business functionality, banks must try to develop WISDOM in the field by acquiring talents and nurturing them in the culture adopted by banks or by training internal workforce to reach the goal. Otherwise, segregating business will be a challenging task.

Risk shift:

In the future, risk functions in banks will likely need to be fundamentally different than they are today. As hard as it may be to believe, the next ten years in risk management may be subject to more transformation than the last decade. And unless banks start to act now and prepare for these longer-term changes, they may be overwhelmed by the new requirements and demands they will face. The structural trends that are driving many of these substantial shifts stem from multiple sources. Regulation will continue to broaden and deepen as public sentiment becomes less and less tolerant of any appearance of preventable errors and inappropriate business practices. Simultaneously, customers' expectations of banking services will rise and change as technology, and new business models emerge and evolve. Risk functions will also have to cope with the evolution of more unique types of risk (e.g., model, contagion, and cyber)—all of which require new skills and tools. Fortunately, evolving technology and advanced analytics are enabling new products, services, and risk-management techniques. At the same time, de-biasing approaches that improve decision making will help risk managers make better choices about risks. However, the risk function of the future will probably be expected to deliver against all these requirements and deal with these trends at a lower cost because banks will, in all likelihood, have to reduce their operating costs substantially.

If banks want their risk functions to thrive during this period of fundamental transformation, they need to rebuild them during the next decade. To be successful, they need to start now with a portfolio of initiatives that balance a strong short-term business case with enabling the long-term achievement of the target vision. Such actions could include digitizing the underwriting processes, use of machine-learning techniques, and interactive risk reporting. They should be complemented by enablers such as a shift in recruiting toward more technology-savvy profiles or the introduction of data lakes. However, to succeed, this transformation could also require a change in the organizational risk culture—the adoption of an approach that embeds shared and communicated values and principles throughout the organization.

The trend of fraud and mounting NPA portfolio is the outcome of the transition phase that banks are going through. This phase is created by Digitalization, Changes in the social landscape, changes in human values, and a lot of other factors. A recent trend in digital capabilities made a level playing field for a bank with a century of existence, a bank with a decade of experience, or a bank with a month of experience. The significant risk is coming out as an existential risk for most of the legacy banks.

To solve all inherent risks, banks must Digitization of core processes, Experiment with advanced analytics and machine learning, Enhanced risk reporting, putting the enablers in place like recruiting correct people, create a data infrastructure for risk mitigation, and enhance risk culture. Most appropriately, we must digitalize all the possible processes which are not under the digital environment must be digitalized, and correct compliance culture must be developed to understand inherent risks report at the appropriate time and take measures instantly.

25

Marketing shift

As a few will visit branches in the near time, our present model of marketing and getting business will soon become outdated. So, this is the high time to capture customer behavioural spending and to analyze data and target our customers. The nature of technological innovations is changing in altogether in a different way than we thought before. Before this age of technological innovations are treated as more of a compliance tool and a tool to monitor and measure performance parameters by managing its back offices, its processes, and its infrastructure. We know these technologies are now impacting the front line- marketing and sales in a profound way.

That is basically due to the process of Digitalization and giving away the operation part, which was primarily performed by our field staff to the customers in an evasive way. Look at the operations in banking, starting from account opening to passbook printing, even the issue of different instruments for operation in the account. Moreover, getting a loan approval does not require so much of interaction. This challenges the very need of consumers to stampede into a bank and demand their work done, so the flow of customers and, in turn, the wisdom of consumer behaviour and their need.

Apart from this, the availability of many a player for their specific job made the system quite inefficient for universal banks. If any customer does require only transaction, he opts for different digital-only banks instead to prefer a full-fledged bank. Those customers are quickly taken away by various players in the market who are playing in the niche market like home loan, vehicle loan small MSME and Agriculture loans. So if you look at the case, most of the customers will pass the banking system to fulfil their needs.

So an urgent need is generated to understand consumer behaviour and involve in the digital methods of marketing our products, which not only fulfil ourselves as a niche banker but this will take advantage of a universal bank. For this reason, we can launch a product named PSB ULTIMATE, which is discussed later.

Bankers now realize that their core asset is their customer base, comprising both individuals and businesses. A well-honed customer management capability—one that enables them to engage, win, and retain customers— will enhance both revenue generation

27

and risk management. Those banks that still have product-defined organizations will have to rethink how they can create a targeted customer-centric orientation rapidly.

Customer insight is the key to success in this shift. Like most other businesses, banks need to sharpen their capability for capturing customer information promptly—for banks; like analyzing their customers' product holdings, cash flows, behaviours, and personal circumstances. The depth of the relationship will be more important than breadth. For example, it will be more valuable for a bank to have an 80 per cent wallet share of 10L customers than a 10 per cent share of 80L customers. More significant wallet share permits greater insight into buying patterns, credit risk, and churn potential, enabling a healthier, more profitable lifelong customer relationship. Customer and decision analytics, which are too often relegated to credit card departments if they are present at all, will now become a critical capability.

Apart from this, a new age of banking is emerging by helping the customers in the value chain. If we investigate the growth of E-Commerce in India, the future of the business community is to align with one or the other, hence competition to get those customers lies with the IT infrastructure or platform we provide to accommodate e-commerce partners. This, in the future, going to play a robust role in marketing those customers. Because to get those customers, banks need capability infrastructure and service standards, look ahead a decade we will lose most of our retail customers if we have not acted upon our capacity building in those value chains.

So, there is now an urgent need for banks to reintegrate the value chain and regain their traditional closeness to the customer to manage risk better and create value.

> If the rate of change on the outside (of an organization) exceeds the rate of change on the inside, the end is near.
>
> Jack Welch

Domain of operation shift

Global regulatory requirement for capital and other supervisory issues draws our attention to reduce NPA and increase profitability. In this globalized and interwoven financial market, the failure of one market affects other markets in the chain in a certain way. So, the pre-globalization era of banking is gone, which gave birth to a new generation of banking with more risk associated with it. Failure of specific industries or markets can damage the operation of banks in our country. Even the routine regulatory change in one country can bring drastic policy change in another.

This phenomenon gave birth to different global regulatory bodies to combat failures. The outcome is merely giving away specific regulatory power to the international community in our own country. The best example is BASEL norms. We need to implement these norms by any means without adopting our methods looking into our asset standards, which might be different from other nations or economic nature of our country. A dip in the US economy can prove hazardous to the Indian economy and, in turn, the health of banks.

30

As the PSD2 becomes implemented, in the EU, banks' monopoly on their account information of customer's and payment services is about to vanish. The new EU directive allows any company interested in eating a bank's share. This change will see many cascading effects in other nations, which is the outcome of globalization.

In the same way, we have seen in the case of cryptocurrency, which led the global front, forcing the Governments to rethink and redesign their strategies.

Technological innovations will be the heart and blood of the banking industry for many years to come and if the big banks do not make the most of it, the new players from Fintech and the large technology companies surely will.

David Brear

Regulatory focus shift

Our regulator RBI is now promoting payment banks, wallets, finance companies. If banks lose sight of customer transaction to other players in the value chain, losing insight it to customer behaviour, in future banks will bear the risk of losing business to these players.

The costs of a failure of the financial system are far more than the costs to the shareholders of the Bank that failed. This is a social externality. Left to their own devices, the shareholders in a bank will underinvest in the Bank's safety from a systemic perspective. The regulatory response to this social externality is to provide government insurance for depositors and, to avoid moral hazard behaviour of these insured banks, to require them to hold higher capital than they would otherwise wish to retain. This response has not addressed interconnectedness directly; instead, it has sought to secure each element in the system.

Thus, an essential function of financial regulation is to balance the interests of unsophisticated consumers of financial products and their sophisticated sellers. This consumer protection focus of law is usually carried out through rules on how products are

32

sold, who can sell them, and, sometimes, what can be sold. Part of the process of consumer protection involves making a distinction between vulnerable consumers and professional investors who are deemed to be less susceptible.

Finance is regulated over and above the way other industries regulated as it exhibits failures in the market that can have devastating consequences. When financial markets malfunction, the real economy takes a nosedive.

There are numerous legislations, rules, and standards that control, monitor, and protect consumers, merchants, banks, and the banking system. Interestingly, regulation is also challenging for all the players in a particular since regulatory frameworks are continuously altering. So what makes the statutory changes? The reasons are to increase competition in the market, to protect the consumers and finally, to prevent financial crime.

As the PSD2 becomes implemented, banks' monopoly and the customer's account information and payment services are about to disappear. Account Information Service Provider, who has access to that account information of the bank customers. They could analyze your spending behaviour or aggregate your account information from several banks into one overview. The other type is the Payment Initiation Service Provider, and they can initiate payments on behalf of the account holder. A bank customer can give the right to a third-party payment provider to make payments from his bank account. This creates competition in the payment area and reduces the price of making a payment or improves the data that you get as a customer. So from a customer and a third-party provider's perspective, this is good.

Another regulatory change is P2P lending. P2P is lending money to individuals or businesses through a platform service that matches lenders with borrowers. P2P credit generally operates online and has served in lower overhead costs and can, therefore, provide cheaper lending than traditional financial institutions. As a result, lenders earn higher returns, while borrowers can borrow money at a lower rate. Even after the P2P lending company has taken a fee for providing the matchmaking platform. Crowdfunding is the practice of backing a project or a venture by raising monetary contributions from many people.

34

Capital requirement hunger

Capital is now recognized as a critical asset strategically and needs to be managed per se. As capital is a major driving factor for banking business, we need to develop our risk management system, diversifying risk to regulatory retail (Risk Weight: 75%), good rated corporates, and Housing loan. Also, increasing profit through non-interest income is a good move.

But it won't be enough to manage capital strategically. Banks must also effectively communicate their strategy to investors, particularly as they seek to expand. Big is no longer beautiful unless it leads to a firm that is better aligned with its core value proposition and delivers an attractive, sustainable return on capital. Shareholders will no longer tolerate empire-building for its own sake. Still, they will long to see a compelling business case for each Merger and Acquisition deal, as well as subsequent reporting around deal performance. Shareholders will also expect to see how specific arrangements fit into a broader M&A and capital management plan that includes divestments as well as acquisitions.

The low-risk, high-return proposition that the banking sector implicitly promised investors has proven illusory. Banks can no longer afford high dividend payout ratios or use leverage to generate oversized returns on equity. Shareholders are now presented with a less attractive, although arguably more sustainable, an opportunity that can best be summarized as "low risk, low return, but low volatility too." Banks need to set and manage this expectation proactively.

So there are two significant areas to be looked into – Strategic management of risk-weighted assets and customer confidence. For this, banks need to think of their orientation and focus on the quality and scale of business while adopting the changes required to sustain in this fast-changing technology customers and market.

CHAPTER 2: TOOLBOX FOR TRANSFORMATION

- ➢ COMPLIANCE
- ➢ IDENTINOMICS
- ➢ DIGITALIZATION

या देवी सर्वभूतेषु वद्यिा-रूपेण संस्थतिा,

नमस्तस्यै नमस्तस्यै नमस्तस्यै नमो नमः॥

"Ya Devi Sarvabhuteshu Vidyarupena Samsthita

Namastasyai Namastasyai Namastasyai Namo

Namahॐ"

COMPLIANCE- Keystone Habit for Organisational Transformation

One of my friends consulted me for his worries, which included deteriorating health to mild depression with a melange of confusion. By going through his issues, I suggested him to read at least one hour of a few good books daily before you go to sleep. His surprise was genuine as reading books has nothing to do with his problems, but with hesitation, he accepted and continued with it. After one month, he called me to say thank you as his state is continuously improving.

Sh Charles Duhigg, in his famous book "THE POWER OF HABIT," described it as "Keystone Habit." Keystone habits pave to the development of many good practices. They start a chain effect in your life that produces several positive outcomes. So in the case of my friend a simple addition of a habit developed other good practices as a ripple effect like a good sleep night, a carving towards the development in the book which led his thought streamlined, his food habit in the night, his sleeping ambience, etc. which in turn reflected in his stress level and other negative habits

38

that were formed in due course of time. Keystone habits say that success doesn't come on doing every single thing right, but instead on identifying a few key priorities and moulding them into powerful levers. Understanding keystone habits grips the answer to the said question: The practices that matter most(keystone) are the ones that, when the habits start to shift, dislodge and remake other patterns.

But when we talk about organizations that developed some habits, it is unlike individuals. Individuals have habits; groups have routines. Routines are the organizational analogue of habits. These kinds of habits seemed dangerous, and we were ceding decision making to a process that occurred without actually thinking. The best banks understood the importance of routines. The worst ones never thought about it, and then wondered why no one followed their orders.

To understand this behaviour, we must understand how brains work. As we can't order people to change, and that's not how the brain works. So we must start by focusing on one thing. If we could start disrupting the habits around one thing, it would spread throughout the entire company.

Considering the case of PSB, we may have to account lots of factors that affected us in a complex loop of habit formation, say routine formation. The factors which are more critical, like the vast cultural landscape of operation, changing style of management functioning, the massive network of branches, and substantial human power in different strata of decision making involved for running the organization.

Now looking into the complexity, we need to be very careful in choosing keystone habits for organization. The habit must be significant and preferably new to the system of functioning and somehow disrupting and appealing to the mass as a whole. For this, if we consider the method of compliance functioning in our Bank, it is still at a nascent level, which can be picked up for keystone habit formation.

40

Compliance function emphasizes on sticking to the regulatory guidelines and internal guidelines at large. But to widen the scope, this can be attributed to every purpose of the Bank from customer service to lending decisions. Briefly speaking, what we are expecting in PARIVARTAN can be easily included in routine formation. Moreover, the act of being complied benefits all stakeholders involved in the process, the staff at large and so the unions and management. This will create a synergy level on performance and overall growth of the system. For example, reaching office before 15 minutes of opening time is well covered in guidelines or maintaining turn around time for each operation well envisaged in codes and internal circulars. This, in turn, develops a culture that is uniform across geographies and personnel in a codified format. Once the routine is formed, it will be hard to break, and in turn, we can effectively implement business-oriented policies.

Let us cite one small example. Most of our accounts are not data sufficient, which affects us in a more significant way when we talk about marketing, future preparation for data mining, and

41

recovery of loans. If this routine is implanted, we not only save time but also prepare ourselves for future challenges in banking parlance. This focusing on one aspect can produce a ripple effect on many other things we might be doing in the wrong way.

THE BALLADS OF PAUL O NEILL OF 'ALCOA.'

ALCOA- Aluminum Company of America was the most promising company in the field of aluminium in the '80s, which produced a wide range of products from a can of coca-cola to bolt used for holding satellites together. But in due course, the sale started stumbling, and the profit hampered a lot. Then the management picked up one pro regulator Govt Buerocrat for the top post. Before taking charge, Mr Neill has gone through different aspects that cause the companies behaviour and caused the loss. He noted one crucial point and made his top priority – SAFETY and took an ambitious goal of zero injury company.

O'Neill believed and understood the key to protecting Alcoa employees, what are the causes of injuries in the first place. And to understand why injuries happened, he had to study what are the flaws in the manufacturing process. To understand weaknesses, he had to bring in able people to educate workers about quality control and most efficient work processes, so that it would be easier to do every work right, since correct work is also safer work.

O'Neill's safety plan, in effect, was modelled on the habit loop. He identified a very simple cue: an employee injury. He instituted an automatic routine where any time someone was injured; the unit head had to report it to O'Neill within 24 hours and present a plan for making sure the injury never happened again. And the reward was: The only people who got promoted were those who embraced the system.

This changing priority not only motivated employees to work in the regulated frame but started giving feedback, which improved the system continuously. The effect is reflected in all spheres of functioning, which was launched from a simple keystone habit of SAFETY. These ultimately saved staff hours, strikes, and material for the company, which in turn turned out to be a profitable factor for the company as a whole.

If we focus on changing or cultivating keystone habits, we can cause widespread shifts. However, identifying keystone habits is tricky. To find them, we have to know where to look. Sensing keystone habits means searching out specific features. It(Keystone habit) offers what is known within academic literature as "small wins." These small wins help other habits to flourish by creating new structures, and they establish cultures where change becomes contagious.

It is not about the new users,
it is about the repeated users
that you can attract.

Dinesh Agarwal

IDENTINOMICS: Seamless Integration of future and Present

If we go by the definition provided by the Cambridge Dictionary, intelligence can be defined as "the ability to learn, understand and make judgments or have opinions that are based on reason." Human beings, by their genetic makeup, are capable of reason. Human beings, throughout centuries, evolved itself by gathering knowledge and utilizing various objects of the universe to satisfy its objective. The Discovery of fire was the first significant achievement of humanity of controlling nature. Then the discovery of wheels and eventually electricity changed the way we lived.

Such inventions are meant to be comfortable and using more and more resources available in the universe. Since then humanity has seen improvement in transportation, medicine, Finance etc. In almost all sectors, humans invented machines to do work which consumed immense labour and thus increased productivity and easiness.

46

In the process of evolution, human beings achieved its value addition by way of thinking, inventing, and knowledge sharing. Simultaneously the machines evolved according to the need of human beings. For instance, wheels developed to spacecraft, and the primary form of energy (muscular energy) evolved to nuclear power. If we look into the universe of things, we can see there are humans working and side by side machines which enhance productivity and comfort.

Then came the digital revolution; we can name it Digitization. In this process, we moved services and data into the computer and made it online, and what changed were the enormous advances in computing power and networked connectivity which have allowed a much more widespread use of digital technologies. In this process, we can collect data in vast quantities and are also capable of storing these data in offline or cloud-based technology.

Presently a new wave of change is happening where we are no longer just get into the Internet with our smartphones. Devices are now communicating with the consumer, manufacturer, and other

47

connected devices. This is opening new and exciting possibilities in health care, retail, banking, and more. *The future is always within view, and you don't need to imagine what is already there.* This is a huge and fundamental shift even more disrupting than fire and wheel or printing press. When we start making things intelligent (the ability to learn, understand and make judgments or have opinions that are based on reason), it's going to be a significant engine for creating new products and new services. We have cloud-based applications translating data into useful intelligence and transmitting the data to machines on the ground, enabling agile and immediate responses. And the result, bridges become smart bridges, and cars become smart cars. And soon, we have smart cities, and this can be done when you will start to think and develop new things.

Let us assume an example of a driverless car that is imminent shortly. In this process, the combination of sensors and machines equipped with the internet can make this happen to surpass the ability of human beings to be judgemental on driving. The roads that we follow by our cognitive power combined with optical power will be taken over by google maps and identical products. When any obstacle coming into our way, we use our mental faculty to observe its impact and do make a decision that will be surpassed by sensors fit into the machine. On getting such input, the device can control itself, precisely say can decide what to do. This is possible through i) assessing signals through sensors II) analyzing the event III) communicating to other devices paired IV) Taking a decision based on experience or the programmed version of it.

We may coin this as Data Analysis, Artificial Intelligence(AI), Internet Of Things(IoT). If we observe the starting of humanity, everything was prevailing except IOT (on the arrival of the internet) in our day to day life. Still, it is high time for their prominence due to the internet boom and ever-increasing computing power of computers and the methods of collecting data and storing it.

IDENTINOMICS:

The fundamental question that will decide our future is how humans are different from machines we operate. How the marketing style will be different will be a significant question when

49

we compete with devices. Here we are not talking about any war among humans and machines but the conflict among the efficacy of humans and that of devices. The person skilled with computer typing will lose his job to a Robot who is capable of translating voice into words or in the past we have seen a man with good computing ability losing his job to a calculator or an Excel sheet.

The answer lies in focusing on the individuality or emotion of a person. This will lead to the concept of IDENTINOMICS. In the nineties before the advent of Core banking banks, through the agency of their branch staff and managers, they knew their customers individually. They knew who they were and how they fitted in- who their family was and what they are trying to do. After core banking implementation and stress on retail business with a little leaning towards third party products, we have lost that insight we were having. In the previous scenario, we were meeting customer expectations, and now we have shifted our focus to 'getting products out of the door'. In this transition phase, we need to go back to the good old days of principles of banking. This banking can be coined as *IDENTINOMICS*.

This concept can be utilized for various objectives from human resources, marketing, and even big data analysis. We are getting in touch with identity, whether our employees or customers can help us grow and be successful in the future challenges we face.

USE OF IDENTINOMICS IN OUR BANK:

Looking back, before we have developed any important machines to help us in our banking, we used our knowledge and capacity to think to build processes and systems like double-entry bookkeeping, auditing, etc. to solve most of our banking activities. When a calculator was introduced, it took away computing skills. When the computer was introduced, it even took our bookkeeping skill and further when CBS was introduced, it took away most of the skills that were in demand and forced us to open to new skill sets. So, in changing scenario, micro-focus on identity is of more importance. With the digital revolution, it is expected that by 2020, 1.7 MB/sec new data will be created per human being on this planet. This data is coming from not just Facebook, WhatsApp, but

51

from all the sensors we are surrounded by like GPS on the phone, millions of photographs we upload and download, etc. In Indian scenario linking of everything with AADHAR enables data preciseness of marketing and targeting customers of course with the consent of the holder.

As one of the major features of digital technologies and applications is their transversality, this will automatically force institutions to rapidly grant access to several functions of their establishments, increasing the demand for computing power and enhancing cyber risks. Cyber risk management could force banks to improve further the robustness of their infrastructure and computing power consumption. Looking into the trend, we can think of future strategies that will affect PSB and the course of action thereon.

A. HUMAN RESOURCES/RECRUITING/TRAINING:

We must visualize it in topmost priority because of its vulnerability and toughness towards the change process. Skills that are important today will be of no use tomorrow. Out of the 76000 employees, we find most of them will not match the need of the time, so reskilling and acquiring skilled people is essential.

The training methodology must inculcate more features like value, believing, independent thinking, teamwork, care for others which machines will be lacking soon and this will augment working in banks being a service sector.

New skill sets such as business analytics, data scientists, risk managers, cybersecurity officers either be inculcated among existing employees or recruited as per demand. In the recruitment process more, emphasis to be given on empathy with the ability to think than certain skill sets or degrees. Changing the whole set of human resources within a definitive period is not an easy tax to do. Hence, we must adopt progressive strategies fixing the year to do radical changes in the coming days.

The changes can be in the form of developing PSB as a learning organization and thinking organization. Special incentives can be awarded for acquiring skills for future-ready courses which might be reflected in their PAF, promotion, and if possible pay. For creating a thinking organization, employees to be motivated for expressing innovative ideas irrespective of their value addition to the organization, and proper communication to be made to the Employee who thought about it. Bank can develop APP by making tie-up with some universities to provide them certifications that can add value to the Employee in terms of recognition and further employability. Or Bank can promote different courses offered by COURSEERA or Google Analytics Academy with relevance to banking. This not only updates awareness and knowledge towards future development but also develop the ability to think and compete with AI.

B. MARKETING / PRODUCT CUSTOMIZATION/BIG DATA ANALYSIS.

Presently we are going through a data crisis due to our legacy of accounts and staff attitude where proper data is not captured by our system, which makes our journey difficult. So, if we want to take a big data approach, we need to go through the following process. 1. Data collection 2. Data storage 3. Data analysis.4. Data utilization.

To understand its proper implementation, we must divide the data into two groups. Number one group is existing customers where we will do- need analysis and the other as the prospective customer who will be utilized for- lead generation.

EXISTING CUSTOMER:

Data collection: Creating data collection points through various channels such as.

1. Branches.2. Apps banking.3. Internet banking.4. By SMS and emails 5. By credit rating and credit information companies.

1. BRANCHES: The most significant advantage of our organization is our spread of offices across this subcontinent—the only thing we need to spread a culture of data collection through proper engagement of personnel.

2. Apps banking and Internet banking.

This is a more significant opportunity for us as these customers are already onboarded to our facilities. By introducing certain features in our apps can collect a big

55

deal of data which necessarily to be customer-oriented features. These features may include a tax calculator, a financial planner, and a model product that will give a special discount in chequebook charges or something same benefits. We need to think ways which will induce customer interest, and in turn they provide their vital data of income and savings.

3. SMS AND EMAILS. A standard method of data point creation, we can send SMS and request customers for feedback on the services they are getting, and in turn, we collect customer data.

4. CREDIT RATING AGENCIES.

Data required for lending can be collected, which will lead us to zero in on the customers as per their ratings.

5. CREDIT INFORMATION COMPANIES.

A beautiful model for data collection of existing customers like their geographical shift, contact change, credit card, or any other requirements they felt.

DATA STORAGE:

We can contact or follow organizations that follow big data analysis.

DATA ANALYSIS AND UTILIZATION:

The data which can't be analyzed and used for bank products are useless. Let us focus on specific aspects of data utilization. As we have discussed earlier about IDENTINOMICS, the data can give a greater insight into it.

Few uses we can think of:

- Extracting data of top contributors to our business, we can send personalized gifts like calendars, birthday wish cards, etc. requesting for further patronage and extending their cooperation in recommending our brand. This can be accompanied by their requirement listing in a return mail. This will not only help us working in the line of IDENTINOMICS but generate business and address grievances. One of the best ways to pacify aggrieved customers is by allowing them to vent their anger by any communication.

- By extracting data from credit rating agencies will help us in identifying the desired rated customers to be chased. They might be pursued for the primary loan product or any other ancillary products. In case of a cash credit borrower of another bank can be looked for housing Loan.

- Credit bureaus are big data machines working for bankers. Suppose we upon specific agreement, go for portfolio data extraction, say we would like to extract information of our housing loan borrowers above 25 lacs; we get exact credit details of those borrowers. That can be further analyzed for different products like credit card, a car loan (if the car Loan sanction date showing five years backwards), etc. we can track customers and can predict what they want, which can bring us greater success. Besides it can help us predict the default rate going to arise in our portfolio or the possible takeover of the accounts.

NEW CUSTOMERS:

Our website can do wonders for this. Let us put some customer-centric content on our web page and in most cases; we must try to gather vital elementary information by making them compulsory for its access. Or we can tie up with various organizations for inputs. Few websites like Fundoodata.com provide information with a nominal charge. This can be utilized for our advantage.

C. **CUSTOMER SERVICE / COMPLAINT RESOLUTION**:

As the machines in the Robotic process automation(RPA) taking over customer service soon. Adopting Robotic process automation demands banks to rethink their entire organization. Robots offer a substantial level of flexibility as they can work 24*7 and are multitasking. Furthermore, automated systems work more accurately and faster, notably on the so-called industrial tasks reducing operating risk. The human touch value-added tasks would, therefore, be performed exclusively and entirely by the human workforce.

This empathy needs to be put in our operation with higher priority. Most of our customer complains, or inquiries are routed through or expected to be routed through Tele calling mode. But we will find many of the complaints or queries are remarked as "refer to branches" which gives rise to a typical case of communication gap and turns out to be customer dissatisfaction and lesser use of tele-calling mode. So, it is time to think about the revival of this model. Let us put a mechanism which satisfies the end. When any customer calls to our Toll-free communication mode, a layer of back end experts should be put in place after primary contact. The problem which can not be satisfactory to the customer must be forwarded to the back-end experts for the solution, and in case the customer needs to visit any unit or branch for resolution of his query, the said unit or department to be informed about it in advance by any communication mode regarding the problem and the ways to resolve the issue. The empathetic approach and human touch must be inculcated in our communication, and this above model will pave the way for it.

D. CREDIT DISPENSATION MODEL/RISK MANAGEMENT:

By the ability of computing power and having enough data on customer behaviour, our credit and risk model can be specifically designed in terms of area wise, product wise, or even customer wise. Many more risk mitigants can be developed using Big Data, AI, and IoT.

For example, in our credit dispensation model, pre-sanction and post-sanction visits are a significant part which till now mostly dependent on the officials involved in credit dispensation. We can develop one application/tool in mobile-based cloud computing where we can precisely locate the place of visit and even capture essential photographs. This will give us quality MIS data for monitoring and taking decisions by inculcating in various tools used by banks like PMS.

E. VIGILANCE/SECURITY/CYBERSECURITY/COMPLIANCE:

When machines are communicating with other devices or processes, it becomes very easier to locate any type of anomaly happening around us.

Let us examine a simple case of Cash Balances maintained by our branches. We can monitor this centrally by enabling AI of our computers by some programs. If the cash balance remains high in an office for a period that is not commensurate with the past trend, then we can put it in a high-risk category and seek human intervention. This will solve any anomaly even before the incidence is about to happen and can save the workforce and money involved to do the same.

Another example can be cited from the process implemented by one of our circles where the model of IoT and analytics applied for security purposes. In that case, all security cameras, CCTV storage, ATMs, cash van, etc. are connected via the internet where they communicate with each other and central server continuously placed at Circle office. If there is an anomaly happens, it reports to the In-charge of security for necessary action. Besides, it ensures healthy functioning of units as machines to communicate with vendors. Apart from a healthy functioning system, this can act as surveillance of branches for better customer service and other related utilities.

CONCLUSION: We are not foreseeing the future, but we are in the future, it is all about our way of visualization. The society is witnessing the most significant paradigm shift in the history of humanity. Through time, humans have acknowledged robotic and monotonous tasks as the standard. But, technology can set us free and allow us to get back to being human and using our imagination and creativity. Both machines and humans have strengths and weaknesses; when we both concentrate on what they are best at, we will see real progress. Let us get some of the vision statements of some of the leaders in the field of the future.

I'm not worried about machines that think as people, I worry about people who think like machines. We need to work together to introduce technology to humanity.

Tim Cook

Any product that needs a manual to work is broken

Elon Musk

It's more profound than I don't know electricity or fire. [While fire is good] it kills people, too. They learn to harness fire for the benefits of humanity, but we will have to overcome its downsides, too.

Sundar Pichai.

We are witnessing the creative destruction of financial services, rearranging itself around the consumer. Who does this in the most relevant exciting way using data and digital wins.

Arvind Sankaran

ॐ सर्वेशां स्वस्तर्भिवतु ।

सर्वेशां शान्तर्भिवतु ।

सर्वेशां पुरणंभवतु ।

सर्वेशां मङ्गलंभवतु ।

ॐ शान्तिः शान्तिः शान्तिः ॥

ALTERNATIVE LEARNING METHOD

In this rapidly transforming business ecosystem, knowledge and acquaintance with developments continuously and effectively is the game-changer. So do we believe that we are fully equipped with this? To answer this question, we must recognize the pace of development and pace of learning and the availability of methodology for that. Digitalization changed the way we are disrupted, and the very nature of Digitalization transformed all the processes procedures adopted rapidly. And if we look into our organizations especially PSU banks the learning curve is almost flat which makes us not up to industry level but allowing us not to believe in the changes that are happening and how to visualize the dangers they pose in front of us. If this lacks in the management cadre, it hinders all the policy-making, implementation of the policy, and finally percolation of not so sustainable vision to the lower strata of organization. Now coming to the different methods to increase the knowledge base of an organization specifically PSB is 1. Hiring from market 2, training at diverse internally setups 3. Training from outside institutes 4. Teaching through different inhouse applications in mobile or else.

67

All these modules face limitations of its kind. On discussing these let us focus on new entrants, once we recruited one officer who has a specialization in Human Resources, the very speciality is disrupted by lots of market developments, for example using analytics in hiring and promotion. And when time passes, we find the skill we acquired of no use. Second, the internal setups which is supposed to reset skills of the employees have a capacity limitation as well as the skill up-gradation of the trainers itself coupled with the constraint of teaching the whole Bank multiple times in a year. The third method of training of employees by outside institutes can not be so useful as they involve huge costs, as well as this, has a limitation of scale. The fourth module is more effective and scalable but having boundaries of contents, research, and innovation.

So how we will solve the issue which is inherent to the nature of Public Sector Banks where so many hurdles exist which includes lack of inertia, alternative decision making fuelled by a legacy system of unions. The answer to this problem lies in a method which is *updated regularly, by experts, have scalability and cost-effective.* So we need to look forward to the set up which provides this in the market. On searching, we can find certain learning startup companies or some companies with specialization. To name few institutes like **COURSERA, LINKEDIN** is providing world-class courses starting from Data science to Management decision making, which has the credibility of world-class universities like ISB, Michigan, and Stanford. Let us understand little about *COURSERA* in a bit of depth.

In 2012, Coursera was founded by two Stanford Computer Science professors who wanted to share their skills and knowledge with the world. Professors Andrew Ng and Daphne Koller put their courses online for anybody to take and taught more students in a few months than they could have taught in an entire lifetime in the classroom. They have 164 partner institutes across 29 countries, offering 2960 courses ranging from Data Science to Humanity.

This has facilities for small and medium organizations to purchase courses in bulk with very nominal and cost-effective prices. Like USD 400 per person per year to USD 110 per person per session. The modules which are taught using audiovisual, texts, news, etc. for better learning experiences.

So adopting these models of teaching in an organization and especially to the executives in PSB not only enhance their knowledge but also make them updated about the developments around the world and this, in turn, can percolate down the line to every Employee of the organization. This, once effectively implemented, makes a knowledge wave that will help in transformation in a financial organization and the primary weapon will be KNOWLEDGE.

We are witnessing the creative destruction of financial services, rearranging itself around the consumer. Who does this in the most relevant exciting way using data and digital wins.

Arvind Sankaran

IDENTINOMICS as a tool for HR transformation

Rapid Digitalization and regulatory strictness moved us from one layer of the regulatory environment to the other. The fundamental principle of KYC shifted from obtaining identity proof to maximization of knowledge about customers, and the requirement of Big data-driven us further to collect customer consumption patterns and customer behaviour both social and with Banks.

The same transformation is also required in our human capital, which is one of the primary inputs for our business. The time is to acknowledge our employees more than that of our customers which can be termed as KYE (know your Employee) in the line of KYC (Know Your Customer). The primary purpose of KYE is to collect data about employees from all the dimensions possible and then analyze it for better utilization and behaviour prediction.

Let us take one example, if we try to find out details of a particular employee reference number, we have a few information regarding him namely geographical information, contact details, transition details, promotion details, award and punishment details, training details, etc. and most of these details are generally routine which is captured in HRMS(operating system for HR management) after the occurrence of the event in a particular sequence. But this does not give rise to the full picture of an employee. Looking into the ability of our system to collect, store, and analyze data about an employee in a broader outlook. We can think of receiving the following information namely

- Hobbies of Employee
- Favourite books
- Banking topics on which employees have a particular interest or have special skills.
- How much credit proposals sanctioned or recommended in a specified tenure
- Contribution regarding Liability product at a particular period
- If posted in other offices, quantified performance parameters if any.
- Credit history from Credit Information Companies.
- Social media profiles like Facebook and LinkedIn etc.

- Other personality parameters from his superiors or colleagues like temperament, handling difficult situations, attitude, etc. on a scale of 1 to 10.

These points can be extended depending upon different situations.

Once we get all of these data about employees, we will be able to use this in the following manners.

- We may use this in deciding postings in sensitive areas, Promotion processes etc.
- We may differentiate employees in different parameters.
- Managing people risk
- We may prepare an attitudinal profile of employees for further correction through training or counselling etc.

All the collection of data to be done preferably through the system as far as possible. Like if we can collect the Facebook profile of employees, it will be very much more comfortable to predict their personality patterns. If we can receive total credit sanctioned by a particular employee, we can take various decisions depending upon the said data, and this is very quickly

73

possible by importing data from the Core server with a marker like employee PF number to the HRMS portal.

Using KYE and digital processes for transforming learning

Proper learning is an outcome of empathizing with corporate goals, thinking, and acquiring knowledge. Anyone factor missing leads to the product to be diluted from its motive. To deliver these aspects accurately, we need data of employees who are exposed to the field.

The process of KYE described earlier gives us a clearer picture of an employee and his training needs. Now, as we are following methods of recording duty sheets in HRMS, it makes the whole process easier. Taking help from these databases, training needs can be formulated and addressed adequately. Apart from it, we can follow up on the process of utilization of the said employees through algorithms in HRMS. Again this training system can become more focused on value training, attitudinal shift apart from creating a sense of belongingness to the organization.

To make the Bank as a thinking organization, we may develop a well-built process. Now to further propagate the spirit of thinking and innovating, we must recognize the effort of the staff in a way or the other. Hence, we can develop a training program for those people who have participated in the process. The workflow of this training process can be like this,

- Collect information about the employees who have actively participated in the process and prepare a database.

- Arrange a short duration training program, namely – INNOVATION QUEST in training centres across the country.

- Call them in groups for training by giving prior intimation about the objective of the program.

- Brainstorm in the program and publish the outcome.

- Highlight the activity in our circulars and reward those participants.

This will not only add value to our product but also motivate employees to be a part of the transformation of the Bank. The moral of the employees, if taken for a higher standard, will produce more top results. Apart from it, it will help to build the KYE process, which will distinguish the employees who have higher motivation towards the Bank and to those of indifferent attitude in turn help bank to take various decisions.

Digitization of the processes in HR

Of late, we have digitized most of our processes performed related to HR functions, which includes leaving, PAF, expenditure on employees, etc. But further scope of this point is unlimited. What we need to think is list down all the aspects performed in HR and make them digitize. Few examples of such exercise may be noted as follows.

- Create an algorithm to record duties performed during tenure of an employee like no of accounts opened, loans sanctioned or recommended, and any other quantifiable performance, if any.

- As per BASEL norms, we have to provide capital on a higher rate if the superannuation benefit is less than the loan amount sanctioned. As the superannuation benefit changes every month, it is a very daunting tax to update the same in the CBS system. Hence if we calculate the said data automatically in HRMs and import it to the staff loan accounts, it will reduce our risk-weighted assets and, in turn, save capital for the Bank continually. Eg. There is an average increase of Rs 50000/- per Employee per year in superannuation benefits. So for approx 50000 employees, it will turn to be Rs 250 crore (Rs 50000*50000) where we can make an impact on our Risk-Weighted Assets(RWA).In rough calculation Rs125 cr(50% of 250 Cr) can be saved each year which corresponds to capital conservation of Rs14.37 crore(11.5% of 125cr).

- Many more processes may be thought of, and the same must be implemented to free up space in banking, which will improve quality and allow us to focus on more critical aspects of banking.

DESIGN THINKING

The banking sector, especially PSBs, is going through a period of interruption, but this will not mark the end of the industry. Instead, this interruption marks the beginning of the banking sector's new DNA, which is a combination of changes in business models, agile execution, and design thinking. When we apply innovation in people, products, and processes in our organization, we can think of two approaches. The traditional method is to design a product out of ideas created by a few. PSBs, instead of focusing on the consumer experience, they tend to develop products to meet their internal procedures and working competences. They tend to put a pretty cover on the product and conclude. And the second method is applying the principles of design to the way people interact with the world. In this case, all employees, including the lowest in strata, regardless of their role, need to perceive themselves as a designer that contributes to refining the customer experience. Discovery of raw consumer sentiment will often yield a product or service that customers love.

78

Financial institutions wonder why so many consumers get frustrated — e.g., customers abandon the online account opening half-way through the process; the actual usage rate is too low. This doesn't meet the user's requirement or address the user's problem or the difficulty they face in using it. This happens when we are not empathizing with customers. Traditional strategy has given us, robust analytics, essential data to make the most logical of decisions about to move in the future. *Design thinking gives us curiosity*. Curiosity has the capability to get deep into the business and find new solutions to traditional problems. It also provides us with the power to observe. Design Thinking solves the problem associated with the conventional designing of products.

Design Thinking goes through the following steps for idea generation and its successful implementation. The steps are 1) **Empathize-** Researching to develop knowledge about what your users do, say, think and feel 2) **Define-** Combine all your research and observe where users' problems exist 3)**Ideate- We need to** brainstorm a range of crazy, inventive ideas that address the unmet user needs 4) **Prototype and testing-** using the insights to generate real product for experimentation and improvisation.

For solving problems coming out of disruptive innovations in the market, banks used to create innovation labs manned by selected employees to ideate innovate and implement products and processes. But these often lose its shine as most of these ideas are never tested on psychological beliefs or empathy of customers who are going to use it. For this implementation of Design Thinking in these innovation Labs is much more essential to give the desired result. So the critical point is Innovation Lab plus a model of design thinking.

Let us look around and find its use in our organization. We are implementing this principle on the go recently in the name of Mission Parivartan – an essential tool for transformation.

Lions Den: A tool for Design Thinking

A few months back, our Bank launched a division named as Mission Parivartanheaded by a General Manager and comprising a team of officers. It was designed as a think tank for the organization. After this Bank launched a portal called Lead The Transformation, where views of all the employees were called

80

for in a mission mode to be utilized as a transformation exercise, this model is nothing but a model of design thinking. Let us understand the steps taken by our organization.

1) **Empathize-** Employees irrespective of cadre working in a bank have the wisdom of customer behaviour, which is a result of both using the product personally and handling customer behaviour in their work, which can result in empathizing customers. The feedbacks, solutions received from employees count a lot while prototyping or modifying a product. If we ask why one of our products has less use, we will get several responses from employees, which is worth accepting. This means customers are facing the same problems, too; if we don't act, then we must take the product out of the market as it might cause collateral damage.

2) **Define-** In this process, our department collects all the ideas gathered and combine and observe where users' problems exist. After thoroughly going through, we define the problem.

3)**Ideate-** In this process, we brainstorm a range of crazy, creative ideas that address the unmet user needs and found out the set of best possible solutions.

4) **Prototype and testing-** After ideation and a more unobstructed view of the problems and solutions, this is sent to different divisions for using the ideas to generate real products for testing and improvisation.

The aim of education must be the training of independently acting and thinking individuals who, however, can see in the service to the community their highest life achievement.

Albert Einstein

DIGITAL GATEWAY: Deciding One Product To Penetrate Digital Arena

When we talked about the Digitization of processes and Digitalization as a whole market wave, we need to talk about digital customer self-service. In this mode of digital development, customers can be accommodated into our digital platform by self-service by following regulations in this regard, and after onboarding of the customer, we must create a gateway for availing the whole bunch of products and services.

Let us understand what a digital gateway is described in this context. Digital portal is a particular chosen product that is so securely crafted by complying with regulations that all the digital products in the offering can be routed through it. Take an example of a customer visiting our brick and mortar office for opening of an account. We have two options to digitalize the customer. The first option is to equip the customer with all our digital products fully. The second option is we will provide our customers with one digital product (gateway product) and educate him on the process to navigate further to our other products through this. If we make

83

the debit card as our gateway product, then link all other digital products and services to be activated through this product. That means by using all the security features provided in the debit card; the customer can self service his other digital requirements of M-passbook, Internet banking, Mobile banking and wallet applications, etc.

So in this way we are getting the following benefits

1. Load on the branches becomes less, and an increase in customer satisfaction.

2. Practically it becomes difficult for branch people to provide all products in the first meeting itself to the customer. Hence failure rate of digitalization is higher for the particular customer.

So modus operandi is equip customer with a digital product (gateway product) and educates the customer on how to proceed with it for a bunch of products and services. The process of education can be done via personal counselling, pamphlets, videos, demos etc.tentative products can become a gateway product that might be Debit card, mobile banking, internet banking, etc.

DIGITIZATION OF THINGS: USING INTERNET OF THINGS

We have heard about the Internet of Things (IoT), which enables machines to talk with robots and humans. We can leverage the solution provided by IoT in our banking services to improvise upon Security and customer services. The project TRINETRA can be developed in our Zone Lucknow for greater transparency and management effectiveness in issues arising from Security, customer service, and HR.

PROJECT OVERVIEW:

All the equipment related to security can be connected to the internet and then to a centralized server, which will do the following things.

1. Monitor system failure.

2. Monitor hardware failure.

3. Monitor vendor and Turn Around Time(TAT).

4. Monitor conflict in branches.

5. Monitor customer service in branches.

6. Monitor human resources in branches.

85

7. It helps us in the collection of Big Data to analyze and put proper corrective measures in those areas.

MANAGEMENT DECISION MAKING:

In simpler words we can give one identical IP address to each security equipment such as

1. Security cameras.

2. Hard Disk of CCTV

3. Onsite ATMs

4. Offsite ATMs

5. Cash Vans

6. Fire Alarms

7. Strong room panels

8. Biometric authentication machines placed in secure rooms etc.

This equipment, in turn, send us data via the internet, which can be centrally monitored and viewed at CO/ZO level.

CO/ZO users can view and analyze the following things:

a. The number of security equipments are functional.

86

b. Any defect in the system, if any, what is the TAT taken by vendors to resolve it.

c. Ambience of the branch.

d. Customer footfall and human resources utilization. Etc.

Benefits to the Bank:

1. Compliance with security is strictly adhered.

2. As branches are closely watched by authorities, there is a scope to analyze and improve customer service.

3. Staff behaviour and attitude are self-controlled, which in turn improves customer service.

4. Guidelines of BCSBI, IAD, RBI, etc. can be complied with and strictly monitored and

5. Productivity can be enhanced.

COSTING:

Approximate cost incurred to implement this project falls as security up-gradation in the Zone. The details of price and agreement and technical aspects are attached. Maximum capital expenditure per circle will Rs 5.0 lacs with existing hardware and recurring spending approx. Rs 20000/- month.

87

FURTHER SCOPE:

- We can manage strong room operations with biometric authentication as well as all our locker customers can be taken into the biometric fold, thus reducing any scope of manipulations.

We can use evolving technology such as face recognition and counting persons who are entering branches or ATMs. This, in turn, provide useful data for analyzing staffing pattern and productivity.

By partnering with Fintech startups, banks will give their account holders the right measure of security and speed. Account-holders can know their money is safe, and they can enjoy the latest financial technology. This is the way to become a digital bank.

Chris skinner

Mobile apps and the use of Google for enhancing features.

In today's world mobile is gaining its momentum to replace Branch banking, physical cards, and chequebooks. Even browsers are replaced by apps. So, in this juncture, emphasizing apps is of greater importance.

So, to remain in the competition, we need to analyze our stand and strategy for better presence. Let us consider the standing of our applications by taking data from android users as well as IOS users. Let us analyze how users rate us and comment upon us. Only by doing so, we will find our faults and can think of new strategies to beat the heat of competition.

Data extracted from android apps rating:

Data extraction:

https://pro.similarweb.com/#/appcategory/leaderboard/Google/356/FINANCE/AndroidPhone/Top%20Free.

On analyzing apps ranking on android phone, the following conclusion has arrived. As on 15/11/2017.

PNB

ANDROID RANKING	APPLICATION NAME
47	PNB mBanking
130	PNB m-passbook
175	BHIM PNB
487	PNB GENIE
621	PNB Kitty
671	PNB MobiEase

SBI

6	Sbiany where personal
22	Sbi card
53	Bhimsbipay
103	Sbi quick
116	Sbi smart
244	Yono (unreleased)

OVERALL

1	TEZ
2	PHONE PE
3	HDFC BANK MOBILE BANKING
5	IMOBILE BY ICICI
19	BARODA MPASSBOOK
30	INDPAY BY INDIAN BANK
68	VIJAYA BANK

Whereas different apps from private and public banks are in the top list in the android market.

The following findings can be considered:

1. The reviews by users are not welcoming.

91

2. Reply by apps manager from PSB is not empathetic in review or mostly no reply to the issues.

3. The issues raised were not quickly solved from our end.

4. This negative review causes damage to the product as digital buyers mostly depend upon reviews and ratings.

5. Our mobile banking apps in the apple store has done significant damage for late up-gradation.

6. The app is not user friendly (as perceived by users and apparent from reviews) and we never done anything empathetically to its queries.

MARKETING METHODS COMPARISON:

Top successful apps were victorious by the referral model of marketing with a brand value attached with it like TEZ and Phone Pe, whereas we mostly rely upon branch banking to promote the app. A combination of both can make things more happening. Also, we can try to use the costs associated with this from The Depositor Education and Awareness Fund Scheme, 2014 - Section 26A of Banking Regulation Act, 1949.

ADDITION OF EXTRA FEATURES IN OUR APPS:

If we acknowledge new rules of marketing and PR, we must focus not only on the product but also its promotion part of it. Now using the Geotagging feature in our apps help a lot in giving an advantage over competitors.

For example, to promote the BHIM SHOP feature of our product, we can offer the geotagging features of google to encourage the shop owner's business, and in turn, we get our product successful.

MODEL:

- Geotag the shops which are enrolled for BHIMSHOP and having a current account with us.
- Add this feature in our mobile banking application where the user can get information about BHIMSHOP enabled merchants near him.
- Add a feature of payment directly to the shop.
- If the user taps shops near me, he will be able to find different categories of merchants and their GPS location to navigate to those shops.

93

In this way, our product will have a unique feature to bank upon which not only improvise our current account operations but also friendly to our millions of m banking users.

Pricing of Geotagging:

https://developers.google.com/maps/premium/usage-limits.

Google charges a very nominal rate for using its services of store locator and navigation use, which again depend upon traffic. Hence to use this will prove cost-effectiveness in operation.

Geotagging features on our Internet banking site:

The feature of geotagging can be used to locate our offices by providing navigation facility which is now operational as a locator.

Geotagging in loan processing.

Geotagging of presanction and post-sanction above a specific limit can be done for keeping records of customers business as well as residential locations.

This will help in the following way:

- It will officially create a record of pre-sanction visit.
- Remotely we can access the location.

- In case of the transfer of officers, it will be easier to locate the units quickly.

- Any post-sanction follow-up can be recorded.

- This can be developed in an app that will be strictly used for internal purposes.

Conclusion:

Now, this model is being implemented by PAYTM for their KYC verification method in different shops in mid-December, and they might go for fullfledged implementation of the same. This can be summarised as the web has opened a tremendous opportunity to reach niche buyers directly with targeted information that costs a fraction of what big-budget advertising costs. Instead of one-way interruption, the internet will deliver useful content at just the precise moment a buyer needs it. It is about interaction education information and choice. So, harnessing the potential of the web at large will help us in getting into the business and do what our objective is to do.

CUSTOMER SERVICE- GOING IN A DIGITAL WAY

In Oct 2017, I wanted to admit my kid in a nursery school near my residence. As billion consumers would take the approach, I googled it on the web by searching a keyword of 'nursery schools near me'. To my pleasure, I found out three schools with all details, including distance from my residence as well as contact number.

Among all of them I found Shemrok little explorers impressive one with its brand ambassador Chotta Bhīma and all its amazing pictures on the web. And ultimately, I admitted my Kid in that school. And if I summarize my act as a consumer, Google marketed that product to me on behalf of Shamrock.

Later, roaming on the street, I spotted another school of equal status which was just located in my neighbouring lane, but the deal was done favouring Shamrock.

Let us compare these two schools by their capabilities.

Attributes	School of my neighbouring lane	Shamrock
Quality	Equally Good	Equally Good
Distance	100 meters	600 meters
Marketing Strategy	Nil/Traditional way	Digital way/Google way

The Take Away from this little shopping:

1. When our best/prospective customers participate socially, so should we.

2. I am sending my innovative products in the way customers like.

3. A hoarding is always hoarded by trees, but a social hoarding continuously enhanced by the web.

4. Blogs and bloggers – tapping millions of evangelists to tell your story.

5. I don't like to read your 1000 words stuff, show me something visual.

6. OMG! I can have Virat's signature on my ATM while searching for his latest score.

7. Wow! My Bank teaches me how to operate mobile banking apps on my mobile.

A CURIOUS CASE OF A MANAGEMENT TRAINEE:

While doing a brainstorming exercise with MT 2017 batch at RSC Lucknow, a curious little boy gave an insight into social media learning. His simple idea: why don't we

97

add all our digital products in video format in social media sites like youtube for handholding of customers for going digital. I was very overwhelmed by the power of this little idea and carried out some research on this.

And yes, the idea can turn out to be a grand success for selling our products if we use our efficiency in marketing and PR.

RESEARCH ON YOUTUBE- SOCIAL MEDIA FOR VIDEO:

The data derived from the study on 02/11/2017. The following data shows the way forward:

ATTRIBUTES	BLOGGER1	BLOGGER2	HDFC BANK
Channel	How to Hindi	About Tech	HDFC BANK
Content	How to activate PNB net banking online step to step	Activate PNB mobile banking	Want to change debit card pin online
Published date	20/05/2016	29/03/2017	16/12/2016
Views	434695	16314	102249
Likes	5000	92	239
Dislike	451	31	48
Comments	1284	22	55
Subscribers	705000	357	52973

The above study reveals we have missed out the real-time customer feedback to evaluate our product and going for customer satisfaction. Imagine 1284 comments about our product which is a mixture of both satisfaction and some dissatisfaction and without intervention of any moderator. This potential can be tapped for the benefit of the bank. This also shows the potential of bloggers in social media marketing.

HOW TO DO AND WHAT TO DO:

1. We can open a channel in YouTube considering the legal aspects of it.

2. Put contents that are relevant to customers while advertising our crucial product.

3. We are reaching out to bloggers for business deals in marketing and PR.

4. You tube like sites can be made as a great place to create a rave by creating something valuable that people want to share and make it easy for them to do so—for example, a great empathy creating story of education loan beneficiary.

99

5. We can send a video link for each activity that the customer intends to do, or the bank intends to provide. Like we can send a video link to customers about how to use ATM while delivering him a green pin or detailed procedure of a car loan while receiving application. This visual video method will change the understanding of the customer about the product we sell as well as about the perception of our bank. (Again, thanks to MT batch for this idea.)

TAKE AWAY:

1. Reaching out to customers will be easy. The referral model of business can be improvised by sharing video links in different channels.

2. Reduction in dissatisfaction level and branch visit by gen-next customers.

3. Any dissatisfaction arising out of misunderstanding of technology can be easily corrected.

4. This can help us build an excellent platform for customer feedback and further development in the product or service.

5. It will be a better way to teach our staff members.

100

6. We can annex these links while sending messages relating to transactions or otherwise.

7. Finally, we can build our brand, from a traditional bank to a next-gen technology-driven bank among the stakeholders.

> Status now is not whether you are awake or asleep, it is whether you are online or offline.
>
> Narendra Modi

BIG DATA ANALYSIS AND HOW IT CAN BE USED IN BANKS

When we look back, in the 1990s if we need to calculate our daily calorie consumption we need to take note of our daily steps and then to convert into a calorie, which was standardized by research methodologies. In this way, we need to take note of everything regularly to analyze and find a proper conclusion. But in 2017 simply we need to install a health application in our mobile which records our movement precisely and converts it into calorie, stores data in its memory, and then analyses to get a proper conclusion. So what changed in these years where the science behind this remained the same, is we are capable of collecting more data and store more data and analyze.

This in technical terms coined as big data. There two things that are fueling this significant data movement: the fact that we have more data on anything and our improved ability to store and analyze any data. Big data is used to understand customers and their behaviours and likings better. Corporations are keen to expand their traditional data sets with browser logs, social media

102

data, as well as text analytics and sensor data to get a complete picture of their customers. Big data analytics is the process of examining large and varied data sets, i.e. big data to uncover hidden patterns, unknown correlations, market trends, customer preferences, and other useful information that can help organizations make more-informed business decisions.

Big data is in practice in so many big companies/organizations for improving performance like Walmart, Netflix, Microsoft, royal bank of Scotland to USA govt. Recently elections in the USA and The INDIA has proved its reach and efficacy.

How is Big Data Used in Practice?

These are significant areas in which big data is currently being used to excellent advantage in practice - but within those areas, data can be put to almost any purpose. For example:

1. **Understanding and Targeting Customers.**

2. **Understanding and Optimising Business Processes.**

3. **Improving Healthcare and Public Health.**

4. **Improving Science and Research.**

103

5. **Improving and Optimising Cities and Countries (smart city).**

6. **Improving Security and Law Enforcement. Etc.**

Some Implications in our day to day life:

Big data analysis affects us many ways in and around our digital life. Once we are connected to the world via the internet, we disseminate the quantum of data to the system by means of visiting different websites, our spending habits, and our social behaviour. If we mark carefully, we get an email or a personalized advertisement on our Facebook if we have searched a product in Amazon mentioning the variation in price. This is nothing but you are being targeted as a customer by taking into account of your behaviour on the internet.

So, with the digital revolution, it is expected that by 2020, 1.7 MB/sec new data will be created per human being on this planet. This data is coming from not just Facebook, WhatsApp, but from all the sensors we are surrounded by like GPS on the phone, millions of photographs we upload and download, etc. In Indian scenario linking of everything with AADHAR enables data preciseness of marketing and targeting customers of course with the consent of the holder.

Indian scenario at banking parlance.

In the nineties before the advent of Core banking banks, through the agency of their branch staff and managers, they knew their customers individually. They knew who they were and how they fitted in- who their family was and what they are trying to do. After core banking implementation and stress on retail business with a little leaning towards third party products, we have lost that insight we were having. In the previous scenario, we were meeting customer expectations, and now we have shifted our focus to 'getting products out of the door'. In this transition phase, we need to go back to the good old days of principles of banking. This banking can be coined as IDENTINOMICS. Where individual needs are to be known in advance and instead of pushing products, we must sell what customer needs. This significant tax can be executed with the help of big data analysis. Organically banks do have more data in comparison to any other industry do have, but still we have not started using it. With the vital information of customers, we can sell our products better than any organization can do.

The case of PSB.

Presently we are going through a data crisis due to our legacy of accounts and staff attitude where proper data is not captured by our system, which makes our journey difficult. So if we want to take a big data approach, we need to go through the following process. 1. Data collection

2. Data storage 3. Data analysis.4. Data utilization.

To understand its proper implementation, we must divide the data into two groups. Number one group is existing customers where we will do- need analysis and the other as a prospective customer who will be utilized for- lead generation.

EXISTING CUSTOMER:

Data collection: Creating data collection points through various channels such as.

1. Branches.2. Apps banking.3. Internet banking.4. SMS and emails

5. Credit rating and credit information companies.

3. BRANCHES: The most significant advantage of our organization is our spread of offices across this subcontinent—the only thing we need to spread a culture of data collection through proper engagement of personnel.

4. Apps banking and internet banking:

This is a more significant opportunity for us as these customers are already onboarded to our facilities. By introducing certain features in our apps can collect a big deal of data which mainly to be customer-oriented features. These features may include a tax calculator, a financial planner, and a model product that will give a special discount in chequebook charges or something same benefits. We need to think ways which will induce customer interest, and in turn they provide their vital data of income and savings.

3. SMS AND EMAILS.

107

A standard method of data point creation, we can send SMS and request customers for feedback on the services they are getting, and in turn, we collect customer data.

4. CREDIT RATING AGENCIES.

Data required for lending can be collected, which will lead us to zero in on the customers as per their ratings.

5. CREDIT INFORMATION COMPANIES.

An excellent model for data collection of existing customers like their geographical shift, contact change, credit card, or any other requirements they felt.

DATA STORAGE:

We can contact or follow organizations that follow big data analysis.

DATA ANALYSIS AND UTILISATION:

The data which can't be analyzed and used for bank products are useless. Let us focus on specific aspects of data utilization. As we have discussed earlier about IDENTINOMICS, the data can give a greater insight into it.

Few uses we can think of:

- Extracting data of top contributors to our business, we can send personalized gifts like calendars, birthday wish cards, etc. requesting for further patronage and extending their cooperation in recommending our brand. This can be accompanied by their requirement listing in a return mail. This will not only help us working in the line of IDENTINOMICS but generate business and address grievances. One of the most sophisticated ways to cool down aggrieved customers is by allowing them to vent their anger by any communication.

- By extracting data from credit rating agencies will help us in identifying the desired rated customers to be chased. They might be pursued for the primary loan product or any other ancillary products. In case of a cash credit borrower of another bank can be looked for housing Loan.

109

- Credit bureaus are huge data machines working for bankers. Suppose we upon specific agreement, go for portfolio data extraction, Say we would like to extract information of our housing loan borrowers above 25 lacs; we get exact credit details of those borrowers. That can be further analyzed for different products like a credit card, a car loan (if the car Loan sanction date showing five years backwards), etc. we can track customers and can predict what they want, which can bring us a greater success. Besides it can help us predict the default rate going to arise in our portfolio or the possible takeover of the accounts.

NEW CUSTOMERS:

Our website can do wonders for this. Let us put some customer-centric content on our web page and in most cases; we must try to gather necessary vital information by making them compulsory for its access. Or we can tie up with various organizations for inputs. Few websites like Fundoodata.com provide information with a nominal charge. This can be utilized for our advantage.

CONCLUSION:

Even though we are moving towards a phase where a few people will visit our branches denouncing our style of marketing and the pace is too fast to catch hold. And the time has come to

Brand is just a perception, and perception will match reality over time. Sometimes it will be ahead, other times it will be behind. But brand is simply a collective impression some have about a product.

focus ourselves on alternatives and big data analysis which gives us a more significant opportunity to do the same. We can use IDENTINOMICS to reach the identity of our customers and to connect with them for a greater good

Unified Payments Interface (UPI) - Impact on banks

Unified Payments Interface (UPI) is a system that powers multiple bank accounts into a single mobile application (of any participating bank), merging several banking features, seamless fund routing & merchant payments into one hood. It also caters to the "Peer to Peer" collect request which can be scheduled and paid as per requirement and convenience.

With the above context in mind, NPCI conducted a pilot launch with 21 member banks. The pilot launch was on 11th April 2016 by Dr Raghuram G Rajan, Governor, RBI at Mumbai. Banks have started to upload their UPI enabled Apps on Google Play store from 25th August, 2016 onwards.

Within two years of its launch, we must look at the latest development on this. The circular no NPCI/UPI/ OC- 15C/2017-18 dated 16/08/2018 gives us Guidelines on Interoperability features for all BHIM UPI Apps.

Guidelines on Interoperability features for all BHIM UPI Apps

This circular is in continuation to the merchant onboarding and interoperability guidelines issued by NPCI through Circular 15, 15A, 15B & Circular 35, for all BHIM UPI apps including that of bank and merchant/ third party apps (PSP SDK and PSP Multi-bank).

Following are the mandatory interoperability features for all BHIM UPI apps to be compliant:

i. Send and receive money using any BHIM UPI ID (VPA).

ii. Generate and respond to Collect request from any BHIM UPI ID (VPA).

iii. Generate BHIM UPI QR and Scan & Pay Bharat QR and BHIM UPI QR.

iv. Respond to Intent call on the same phone by any BHIM UPI app or merchant.

A.) The above compliance applies to all BHIM UPI apps, including the merchant/third party apps.

B.) The merchant only apps are excluded to have compliance of the following functionality since their core business is merchant services;

        a. Send money using any BHIM UPI ID (VPA) is optional.

        b. Generate BHIM UPI QR is optional. However, Scan & Pay Bharat QR and BHIM UPI QR is mandatory.

        c. Generate collect request to any BHIM UPI ID (VPA) is optional. However, respond to collect is mandatory.

C.) This compliance does not apply to the merchant apps collecting or receiving payments using BHIM UPI (apps not onboarding/ registering customers on BHIM UPI or not creating exclusive VPA on merchant app).

The above interoperability features must be enabled by 16th April 2018 by all BHIM UPI apps. The other compliance as per earlier circulars shall continue to be applicable.

PSP bank must decline such transactions from non-compliant BHIM UPI apps after 16th April 2018 proactively. NPCI reserves the right to decline the transactions for such non-compliant apps.

The PSP Banks are advised to submit the compliance to NPCI

on or before 16th April 2018.

The regulations regarding UPI are becoming more transforming in the times to come. This necessitates a fundamental question, what disruption it can create in the market? How will banks survive this? Let us discuss the"what" part first.

1. After UPI, customers are free to use any platform of any bank or fintech companies they like. Before the introduction of UPI, if a customer of a particular bank wants to access his bank account, he needed to use any product of that specific bank like a chequebook, mobile banking, wallet, etc. but after the introduction of UPI platform, the customer is free to use any bank or any fintech of their choice which fulfils his requirements or preferences. This change will make all new tech-oriented startup fintech companies and large traditional banks in similar footage. If there is a lesser difference in organization structure, the companies with faster innovation and higher investment in financial technology will be a winner in this level playing field.

2. The second threat from this is regulation changes supporting digitalization. Suppose the regulators make it mandatory for all Banks and fintech companies to share customers data if the customer wishes to do so with its preferred financial service provider then there will be an end in monopoly of bigger banks in the technology field and preferably they will succumb to pressure from all-new generation mobile-only banks like Paytm.

3. The last threat might be the introduction of new players like Account Information Service Providers, who have access to the account information of the bank customers and can provide customers with the insight of financial planning and investment. In this case, banks without these accesses will be lost sight of customer economic behaviour and eventually, all the marketing and customer satisfaction.

The above facts foretells that UPI can lead us to open banking which is much talked in other nations. As a traditional bank, what we must do.

1) We can make the UPI application as simple as possible yet more inclusive.

117

2) UPI module must be integrated with all other applications like internet banking, mobile banking, etc. enabling customers to do transactions easily.

3) We can use different incentive measures to gain popularity and spread among customers.

4) We can educate existing customers to use banks own platform instead of other platforms available. The education must include safety measures to be taken.

5) We can Make customers UPI enabled like capturing mobile number and issuing debit cards. In some cases, we may consider a different product which allows customer can have a **_virtual debit card_** for this purpose for that customer to feel shy about using physical debit card due to maintenance cost or otherwise.

6) Capturing correct data as well as cleaning old data, is an excellent exercise in promoting UPI enabled services in the bank.

7) Tie-ups with Fintech companies and other innovative firms for better display of innovation in the said platform.

Data on UPI adoptation:

118

Year	Transaction Volume (In Million)	Transaction Value (In Rs. Billion)
2016-17	17.86	69.47
2017-18	737.18	856.59

There is no room for complacency in the fast-moving digital world.

Neeliekroes, EU commissioner for Digital agenda.

Digital natives: Banking for Generation Mute

We are facing transformational threat from Digital native customers as well a more significant transformational threat when they become generation Mute. Unlike before the scope of communication has increased a lot via social media where the present generation is communicating with a relatively more significant no of peoples in a brief period. This multitasking habit leads them to use less of their vocal chord. Look at trains busses classrooms even within families the mute mode of communication is more influencing than vocal method of communication. Also I remember calling a friend on his birthday or anniversary becoming a rare event than it was before. Even families prefer to be more involved in social media to celebrate than being vocal. Also, this generation prefers to follow its pursuits like listening to music or watching a video while communicating.

When people change the mode of maintenance of their relationships, we the bankers expect them to be in the line of vocal communication to do their banking. Now the banking for this generation is a job that must be done while listening to music or

120

waiting for the train and without any vocal communication with its banker.

Youngsters simply do not like talking now. Texting or using social media is excellent, even an earphone can do, as long as speaking is avoided. Here is a survey from the British communications regulator, OFCOM, revealed. About 15 per cent of 16-24 years old do not want to use their phones to speak to people. They would rather text. In times magazine mobility poll, 32 per cent of all respondents said they would instead communicate by text than phone, even with the people they know quite well. This is truer still in the workplace, where communication between colleagues who are often not friends. A Nielsen survey says average monthly voice minutes (18-34 yr old) have plunged fro about 1200 to 900 in the past two years and texting has more than doubled from an average of 600 messages a month two years ago to more than 1400 texts a month now. Social media changed the way we communicated privately. There was a time when talking over the phone for hours used to be a relaxation technique between friends, lovers, families but now we think twice about violating someone's space by calling them over the phone. It is also a scientific fact that anxious people become tongue-tied. Now, think about an anxiety-ridden generation, multi taxing 24*7. No wonder even the thought of picking up a phone to talk has become a terror.

Looking into the above scenario, what must be our banking strategy transformation to fit into this all mobile mute generation. The answer lies in innovation and digitalization and investment. The following points might be considered while forming productions for this generation.

1) All mobile banks are best suited for this generation as well as whole banking in a single application platform providing all inputs, products, analysis, on-boarding, and finally, consumption.

2) The information dissemination must be unambiguous and without many hidden messages which needed to comprehend and understood.

3) Use of features like Artificial Intelligence to read the need instead of the customer asks his want. This technique is becoming more famous day by day due to its unique characteristics of machine learning.

122

4) Use of CHATBOTS(A chatbot is a computer program which conducts a conversation via textual or auditory methods).: These programs are often designed to credibly simulate how a human would behave as a conversational partner, thereby passing the Turing test.). This chatbots can solve the muteness problem of this generation. Chatbots will allow customers to converse with machines and explain their everyday issues. AlsoHmanbots (specialists) can be used as a second line of service provider to solve queries beyond machine comprehension.

5) Using social media for payments or the features pay while chat features. Imagine a bank introduces encrypted apps for its customers where all messages are safe and secure and can be communicated among the customers of the bank and while doing communication the customer can pay, send instructions to the bank, etc.

6) Continuous innovation in the field of technology and finally

123

7) Investment in technology. As now banks are shying away from investing in physical infrastructures like brick-mortar branches and ATMs, this investment portion must shift to technology and Trust. Instead, I would suggest investing in Trust and Technology must be a significant portion of total investment by a bank in a period. When we talk about Trust Investment, we understand investment in building a brand, investment in the latest technology for better customer experience, and investment in Cybersecurity for protecting customers.

Almost all quality improvement comes via simplification of design, manufacturing, layout, processes, and procedures.

Tom Peters

IDENTINOMICS: BEACON BANKING AS A TOOL

We all have experienced the marketing style of hotels in the proximity of Railway stations or highway Dhabas where they depute one salesman to offer individual passerby their products. That style is quite natural and effective as all the customers in the proximity were approached personally, which ensured nearly 100 per cent hit. Now in this era of digitalization, how we can use the method of Dhabawala in the banking business. The primary purpose of IDENTINOMICS is to personalize services or products offered to customers and to know the customer needs in advance and to provide a tailored solution. This can be augmented by adopting Beacons in the banking system.

This technology is not a very sophisticated one as compared to Artificial Intelligence (AI) or the Internet of Things(IoT). To understand this, let us Tech-change Dhabawala model of marketing.

- Replace the salesman who is calling customers by a BEACON which is nothing but a sophisticated Bluetooth device sending signals and receiving signals.

125

- Replace the voice of the customers by Bluetooth waves.

- Replace the receptibility of the customer by notification in an APP where he can accept or reject the offer provided by a branch.

Technically speaking the most favourable form of Proximity Marketing can be leveraged via using Beacon technology in banks. With an iBeacon/beacon network, any brand, retailer, app, or platform will be able to understand exactly where a customer is in the brick and mortar environment. This provides an opportunity to send customers highly contextual, hyper-local, meaningful messages and advertisements on their smartphones. The typical scenario looks like this. A consumer carrying a smartphone walks into a store. Apps installed on a consumer's smartphone listen for iBeacons. When an app hears an iBeacon, it communicates the relevant data to its server, which then triggers an action. This could be something as modest as a push message and could include other things like targeted advertisements, special offers, and helpful reminders.

USES IN BANKS:

126

While there is a vast scope in leveraging this technology from Customer service to marketing or collecting customer behaviour for future use, let us put some light on this aspect.

A. Location responsiveness offered by iBeacon technology will allow banks to be upbeat with their customers. E.g., banks can use beacons to integrate the physical branch with a mobile device in the hands of a customer. The moment a customer walks into the office with a smartphone, the bank will be able to recognize her, bring up appropriate information with the teller or bank manager, and equip the bank people to offer proactive services. Or a kiosk-like structure can be provided where customers with Apps can communicate with a machine placed in Kiosk to solve his banking requirements as well as advise him about his future programs by analyzing his past spending behaviours, credit requirements, and income by Artificial intelligence and big data analysis.

B. We can tie up with the merchants where our card is used for some special promotion or offer and can guide our customers regarding this.

127

C. We can design our product so that a person with a particular need can be attended carefully, thus increasing personalized services to the customers.

D. Digital tokens can be issued by using this technology and thus giving a specific timeline for serving a customer. Also, in addition to this, we can provide some learning or entertaining materials to customers for enhancing his waiting experience.

E. The fundamental problem of our system is the customer is confused to get his services due to complexity in structures, ignorance of customers, or non-empathetic staff. By using this technology, we can direct the customer to the specific person for the particular job requirement. For more convenience, internal structural maps (for big offices) can be directed to customers.

F. We can implement this technology in the Head Office for our entire staff who either visit or work there for easy access to information about the location of departments or persons with whom one needs to meet.

Let us cite an example of some of the companies who have leveraged this technology.

1. Retail hypermarket Auchan leverages for wayfinding and more.

2. Google uses over 2000 Beaconstac beacons at railways stations in India.

3. Barclays bank recently leveraged beacons in branch to streamline and personalize bank visits for consumers with disabilities.

4. The Changi Airport in Singapore taps mobile beacons to automate immigration check. Etc.

As on Aug 2017 approx. 92% of Android devices have the capability to be used in this platform. Also, we have digital products in a place like mobile banking, etc. Hence this is easier for us to adopt this technology and leverage it. For this, we must increase our digital reach among customers and specifically acceptability of our technology amongst youth. Unless we might find a situation in the future whereupon entering a shopping mall salesperson from our competitors are calling customers, but our salesman is absent.

Branch Replacement: VR, AR and MR

Augmented reality (AR), virtual reality (VR) and mixed reality (MR) is the foundation of a 4th wave of computing power that integrates sensors, big data, the cloud, artificial intelligence (AI), and wearables. Artificial reality (in the general sense) includes all of the technologies that bridge physical and digital experiences, including augmented reality, virtual reality, mixed reality, and extended reality.

Virtual reality (VR): An artificial environment which is experienced through sights and sounds provided by a computer, and in which a person's actions partly decide what happens in the environment. To replace a user's existing reality with a digital one, VR occludes the user's natural surroundings.

Augmented reality (AR): An enhanced version of reality created by the use of technology to superimpose digital information on an image of something being viewed through a device (such as a smartphone camera). AR lets you see both synthetic light and natural light bouncing off objects in the real world.

Mixed reality (MR): A system that merges real and virtual worlds to produce new settings and visualizations where physical and digital objects co-exist and interact in real-time. Virtual objects are meant to look believable, aiming to take the best combination of VR and AR.

Extended reality (ER or XR): It is a superset of all the technologies ranging from entirely real to entirely virtual. Everyday use cases could be the flying of drones, undersea exploration, or surgical robots.

With a desire for engaging design, simplicity of use, and multichannel support, digital consumers want an alternative delivery alternative than traditional brick-and-mortar banking. Implemented correctly, AR/VR/MR can transform financial data into a visual, engaging experience and can eventually bring the face-to-face experience into a customer's home.

In a digital world, where digital banking channels are growing in popularity and becoming better designed and easier to use, we need to determine whether the consumer *wants* to visit a physical branch or if they simply think they have to? And will the digital consumer accept an interaction in a virtual world as opposed to a material world?

131

Strategy for PARIVARTAN: PSB ULTIMATE

Scientific Background:

Mr Charles Duhigg, in his famous book "The Power of Habit" described Habit Loop governing day to day affairs of human beings. An action is done repeatedly transformed into a powerful habit that is difficult to break. This principle can be used in customer acquisition and customer retention. Let us describe a scientific experiment regarding this.

MIT researchers discovered the habit loop while experimenting with rats running mazes. They found that during initial maze runs, the rat's brains generated a great deal of activity in the cerebral cortex. However, navigating the mazes after numerous repetitions required less activity in the cerebral cortex, even in part governing memory. The brain converts the sequence of actions, chunking them into primitive basal ganglia, reserving the cerebral cortex for higher or more intensive functions. This is the mechanism when we are arriving home, and we have no conscious memory of activity, attentively driving all the turns.

132

Thus, the habit loop is a neurological circle that rules any habit. The habit loop consists of three fundamentals: a cue, routine, and reward. Understanding these fundamentals can help in understanding how to form habits or change it to a better one.

The Cue: It can be anything that activates the habit. Cues generally fall under the following types: a time of day, a location, other people, and emotional state, or an immediately preceding action.

The Routine: A habit's routine is the most apparent element: it's the behaviour you wish to change or reinforce.

The Reward: The reward is the reason the brain decides the previous steps are worth remembering for the future. The reward provides positive reinforcement for the desired behaviour, making it more likely that you will produce that behaviour again in the future. The reward can be anything, from something perceptible (e.g. a personalized calendar), something intangible (e.g. a free music application) to something with no inherent value but what it is given (a special feeling).

Once a customer enters this loop, it becomes easier for us to manage his product choices and especially psychologically to force him to use our product. For this, we need to create a unique product category for the targeted group of customers. Hence, the product PSB ULTIMATE can be utilized to create value in customer experience.

PSB ULTIMATE:

Taking a clue from the above scientific research and well established and adopted theory, we can develop a product for our targeted customers. We may develop an application to attract our targeted customers and onboard them with the product they are currently enjoying and eventually encourage acceptance of other products available. We may collect all the information required for need analysis and serve them all the products they need in a very much shortened TAT.

Basics of the product:

1) The product must be an end in itself. Before onboarding customers into this product category, we must ensure that all relevant data captured by the system and well-analyzed beforehand like creditworthiness, net means, etc. and for

this, we can start from all our non-delinquent retail and corporate borrowers and high net worth individuals.

2) The pricing of the product must be appealing to the customers. People must see value in PSB ULTIMATE in terms of value for money and customer satisfaction.

3) A particular line of tech-enabled post-sale services must be provided to these segments of customers.

4) The product must be mobile-only for sustainability.

We must try to inculcate features of IDENTINOMICS like data analytics, business analytics, and Artificial Intelligence while delivering this product to our customers for enriched customer experience and customer identification.

TARGET CUSTOMERS:

1) They are existing, valued credit customers.

2) They are existing valued deposit customers.

3) Customers willing to share information.

FACILITIES FOR PRIME MEMBERS:

1) Separate application for onboarding or onboarding from any digital channel will be available.

135

2) Dedicated call Centre for grievance redressal and customer experience or technology like virtual reality or chatbots can be utilized for those customers.

3) Facilitation in service will be offered by lowering Turn Around Time.

4) Beacons will be used in identified centres (branches or kiosks) for these customers. The Prime app will be integrated with Beacon listening capabilities.

5) Credit cards will be supplied to customers by customers online request. (As already we have in possession of information. Income-related information can be acquired by a tie-up with the Income Tax department after receiving online approval from customers.)

6) Individual facilities may be provided after looking into cost analysis like

a) Personalized yearly calendar.

b) Free SMS charges, CARD charges.

c) Limited number of free NEFT, RTGS, clearing of cheque, Issuance of Cheque leaves etc.

d) Limited waiver of cheque returning charges.

e) Discounted/free music subscriptions from Gaana, Savan, etc. to attract young generation customers. This can be done by collaboration or purchasing of the said companies.

COST ANALYSIS OF THE PRODUCT:

The following factors need to be considered while fixing the price for the prime customer.

Serial Number	Factors	Value
1	Expected returns from the addition of Prime customers	A
2	Expected loss from freebees calculated by business analytics	B
3	Amortized investment in Information Technology	C
4	If any tie-up with external companies done for services, then the cost component	D

The pricing of Prime customer onboarding to be fixed either by

No impact basis: A>= B+C+D

OR with investment in customer retention by expecting some losses which will be passed on to the customer and the gain can come from either by the scale of operation or from cross-selling of product bucket. Business analytics must be applied at regular intervals to understand the impact of the said product and deciding about pricing and benefits.

FUTURE SCOPE:

Once we grow with our prime members, we can focus on converting loyalty reward points into bank shares to create a feeling of ownership among our customers for whom the bank is reaching new heights.

CONCLUSION:

By creating this product, the bank can route its presence to the very basics of psychology and emotion, and in turn, the bank will get rewarded by customer loyalty and prosperity in business. This covers the basics of IDENTINOMIS of having direct links between Customer and Bank. Some features might be added to strengthen the product as cited below.

Enhancing service factors without losing revenue/opportunity cost:

- Reward points while using the products through App.
- Conversion of reward points while renewing subscription.
- **Live cricket score** or alike products

138

- Bank will greet customers on birthday or anniversary etc.
- **Customers can download Verified/digitally** attested copies of KYC docs, income proof or address proof etc.
- The reward points to be redeemable for shareholdings of the bank if possible.
- There will be a separate call centre for grievances redressal.
- Financial analysis features like tax planning, investment planning.

Offers which includes sacrifice in cost/opportunity cost:
- Free debit card/credit card charges
- Cheque bouncing charges waiver
- Clearing charges to a certain amount
- SMS alerts
- **Music/Movie/magazine** subscription
- Gifts like personalized calendar etc. on special occasions.

Customer identification parameter:
Two distinct approaches can be made-
1) Bank to customers

2) Customer to Bank

Bank to customers:
- Identify by putting different parameters like
  - Average deposit with us.
  - Quality advance
  - Period of relationship
  - Profile of customer by looking at his job, income, etc
  - By extracting credit history of credit customers where the customers are still left with some credit absorption capacity.
  - Different customers using our third party products but without availing credit facilities. Etc More parameters can be brought forward in this method.
- This can be done by visiting different institutions for the marketing of the product.

Customer to Bank
- Our App customers who want to be a part of this process will submit their data for analysis and later on onboard to the product.
  - Direct approach through app downloads.
  - New accounts opened during the period.
  - Tie up with music apps or alike products.

Changing attitude among employees for third party business

Increasing social media activities helped many wrong notions which were circulated among our employees which not only created a withdrawing attitude but also damaged our reputation on different products.

One of these affected products is third party products which are remunerative as well as risk mitigants.

To motivate employees and to build a positive perception about the product, the following aspects need to be inculcated among the employees.

Insurance Business: Changing attitude with a different outlook

Before describing all the benefits because of fee-based income or any other business losses from these businesses, we must ask a question.

If there are no tie-ups with different life or non-life insurance companies, what will be the scenario?

Ans:

1. We will lose our profit coming as commission.

2. We will not be able to cater needs of some of our customers who usually ask for different third-party products looking into the prevailing market business style.

3. And the most crucial part is in the absence of these products how we will insure our credit customers and assets created out of bank funding. Now if we want to insure a customer who availed a housing loan, a single form and an entry in Finacle is enough for this, but if we don't have a tie-up, we will end ourselves in perpetual mess in managing this issue. The same is valid for non-life products also. As well we lose our customers who are supposed to have a long-term relationship due to insurance products. For example, a customer linked with us through any third-party product which may be PMSBY, APY, PPF, or any insurance product tends to extend the relationship for a more extended period which tallies with the life span of the associated product. We have witnessed it in the form of operative accounts when mentioned in IT returns.

If we analyze the above-mentioned objectives, we can conclude that those tie-ups not only make our credit delivery mechanism easier but also act as a tool for improving profitability. To maintain tie-ups, we need to do a certain amount of business;

143

otherwise, the companies will not find value with us. So basically, the above argument necessitates to think the business arrangement another way around—the fundamental question of conglomeration – who needs whom must be looked objectively. And we can conclude that these arrangements are in a win-win situation. Hence our effort will be in that direction. We grow with these tie-ups in terms of quality credit as well as profitability and never to mention new relationships and to retain existing relationships.

Next aspect we must understand about profitability:

Apart from risk mitigants and helping banks in delivering products, these third-party products give us a profit that we are hungry. And this profitability came without any capital requirement or any future risk associated with it.

The Bad roads:

If we look into the aspects, we are conceptually correct about third party insurance business but are we somewhere wrong in implementation. To answer this question, we must comprehend the sale strategy involved in these products. The main culprit of this is Misselling, and the solution is cross-selling. We must stop Misselling as termed as Push sells and promote these products as cross-sells, which not only increase customer confidence but also improve our profitability.

Government business: A source of continued relationship and profit.

Many a product is floated by Govt which are delivered through banking channels, for example, APY, PMSBY, PMJJBY, APY, PENSION, PPF, NPS, etc. If we analyze, these products have many more important features that need to be communicated to the field for better acceptance. Few points can be described here.

1. Generally, Govt. schemes are long term in nature, so providing these to our customers, improving that long-term relationship.

2. A single pension account (with zero QAB) can earn about Rs800- Rs900 which is more than a saving accounts having QAB of Rs20000/- or a fixed deposit of Rs 50000/-. Changing views about this product among employees will build empathy and in turn, compassion and customer service.

3. A simple PMJJBY or PMSBY protects all our loan portfolios below Rs2 L in a very cheaper and efficient way which is quite impossible through insurance products prevailing in the market.

4. A product like NPS paves the way for the customer base for all other arrays of investment products and credit products because of their taxpaying nature.

145

Third-party insurance products generally form an efficient strategical arrangement for improving profitability as well as helps in managing our risk related to credit in an efficient and hassle-free way. Hence, we must take these products as boosters for our credit products and customer experience. One change in outlook for insurance will be a big leap for Bank as a whole.

If banks can not offer something more valuable than Amazon Prime, then we are probably in the wrong business.

Bradley Leimer

Bank Boards: Venture into unchartered areas

Accelerated technological advancement has substantially improved industrial productivity and allowed suppliers to produce an unprecedented array of products. This, in turn, upsurge to a new segment of the industry to grow, the service sector. Now the service sector is almost taking the lead in the economy. This resulted in an increasing number of industries and supply exceeded demand.

As the effect of globalization and liberalization, companies started losing their niche market. Thus, market monopoly began to evaporate. The supply started rising exponentially, but demand remained static (though added by increasing population and acquiring new market places by the help of globalization).

When so many choices with very little difference in product quality presented before consumers, then eventually the price of products took the driver's seat for sale determination. And this leads to a price war among companies and reducing their profitability. This can be seen in the form of discounts offers and other war technologies employed by companies once certain brand names like Xerox, Colgate which made their way to every household are now becoming another brand of photocopier or toothpaste.

In overcrowded industries differentiating brands become harder in both economic upturn and downturn. So, to beat the heat of the competition innovation around the particular product is much more important to create its own space and when this space started crowding, we must move swiftly to other new innovating areas.

Before innovating a product or procedures, we must think of the following aspects.

- Trust or emotional aspects of the product.
- Customer groups or segments.
- Scope of the product with feasibility and complementing output.
- Product that fits a different need of the customer.

Creating your customer segment is much more important to focus on a non-competitive market. This can be supplemented by a non-customer in a phased manner.

The potential to disrupt is enormous because the consumer business in India has been very static for the last 50-70 years. As this business-changing very fast, so do the scope of banking business. Hence, this is the time to look into a new array of products, unchartered territory for our products. This necessitates innovation as well as disruption of the market.

149

For example, simplifying credit uptake for rural areas other than agriculture, we must modify existing schemes to suit for retail products. Collaboration with value chain companies to provide capital for the producers in the chain. Designing customized products for selected individuals. Conjunction with E-Commerce companies for financing their partners is a welcome step for this.

Digital is the main reason just over half of the companies on the fortune 500 have disappeared since the year 2000.

Pierre Nanterme

Transformation in Banks: Strategy

The transformation is a journey of miles together in different seen and unseen paths to achieve a desired result which has no proper definition either. This journey requires various nuances of strategies covering the significant aspects of people, process, and product. For developing a plan, we usually rely on established tested paths and often adopted by peers in the industry or prescribed by management consultants. We'll always need them to understand competitive landscapes and to assess how companies can best deploy their resources and competencies there. But we need to acknowledge that just giving people those tools will not help them break with conventional ways of thinking. We must therefore learn to generate groundbreaking strategies; we must have tools explicitly designed to foster creativity.

Here we will discuss on various strategy formation strategies which will auger innovative landscape. Whatever we see and experience around us in doing business has a fourth dimension. The best way to innovate is to understand this dimension very well. Let us know some thinking processes with one or two examples and then let open the ideas to float in diversified contexts in our banks.

Concept 1: *Defamiliarisation*

Describing objects from a distorted perspective and rebuffing to use the customary names for objects and by generally "making strange'" (are de-familiarizing) the otherwise familiar. When we visualize the world, we should not only scrutinize, but examine with a deliberately different outlook. This includes names what is around us, but come up with new ones. Not just consider the entire, but break things into pieces. These procedures can help us see our way to the latest and the innovative, whether in the arts or business. The other ways we can say pulverize the process and build new.

Application: Defamilarize the role of specialist officers in banks, see the alternative ways they can contribute. Create a duty sheet that will contribute differently. A security officer can be made responsible for security (broadening the duty) at the micro-level. A Hindi officer can act as a translator of relevant banking literature and other communications. A marketing officer can be made a lead customer care officer. At the time of recruitment, some additional qualifications related to a job profile can be looked into so that these qualities can be utilized further. Likewise, we can think of many innovations.

Concept 2: Addition

Look for the independent products and processes in your organization. Calculate the value they are producing. Probably if you find some processes are value consuming, then seek to combine with others to find an augmented effect. Advent of technology made it easier to introduce any combination effect quickly. Trials in these areas take less time and resources due to technological availability.

Application: Management information system adds value to the organization. Marketing strategy formation is also a significant growth engine. Try to combine them. You will have wonders.

Train Your Auditors As Trainers: Make your Auditors as trainers. Work on it. Believe me; you will find results in compliance and accomplishment of goals. The concurrent auditors have continuous access to more than 50 per cent of businesses and people. Training the staff in those fields will be much easier if we train auditors to become trainers.

Concept 3: *Subtraction*

Strategy sometimes needs letting go of the things we have. Find the unnecessary processes in your bank. Pulverize them and make a new set of processes or products and let most of them go. Use technology where ever it can be applied.

Application: Banks tend to confuse customers and employees by providing many products and change them frequently. By doing so, the bank increases the knowledge gap. Let go all this and adopt a few comprehensive products with customizations within that product. This empowers employees and customers to choose what most suited for them.

Concept 4: *Division*

This is the beauty of an organization. Division of responsibility or delegation can cause a conducive atmosphere for creative ideas. The delegated piece of job generates motivation, and accomplishment of it gives satisfaction. But wait what need not to be delegated. Remember a CEO must not delegate Culture. It must not be divided but need to be strongly put together to form

154

unique challenges and innovating. If this aspect is delegated, it creates dark patches in the organization and these patches once formed; it becomes very difficult to go away with it.

Application: PLC (personal learning cloud) is in the leaderboard. Digitalized informations, abridged books, specialized jobs along with scalable technology is the new mantra which is catalyzing innovations in the field of corporate learning. These ideas are leading the startups to create platforms and channelize demand and supply. These models can be used or created. But what are the steps to be taken! 1- Pulverise the knowledge required by employees by job description. 2- Reconstruct the need for a particular job by defining it. 3- Create knowledge fragmented-functional, technical, behavioural, managerial, self-developmental, and leadership related. 4- Create online materials specific to the role and properly fitting to the fragments mentioned in point 3. 5-Help employees avail of these when they require it. 6- Use IDENTINOMICS to monitor and evaluate.

Concept 5: Multiplication

Banks need the power of scalability. This can be achieved through digital transformation—technology-enabled organizations to produce digital goods and services at a very cheaper and faster rate. But Digital Transformation Is Not About Technology - Strategy, culture, and customer experience are just as important. Digital transformation worked for few establishments because their leaders went back to the basics: they focused on changing the mindset of its affiliates as well as the organizational culture and procedures before they decide what and how digital tools to use. What the members foresee to be the future of the organization drove the technology, not the other way around.

Application: Today, PSBs are struggling for filling the knowledge gap, leave alone behavioural learning. To begin with, we need to ask a fundamental question to ourselves, where is knowledge? The answer is in every walk of life, anything we do, in our mobile phones, in our emails. Virtually it is present everywhere. To allow the employees to learn is to stimulate the pattern only. To encourage, we need to give incentives and to open specific channels for this. One of the channels might be developed by our own or accept channels developed by others. MOOCs (massive open online courses) help you to get there with no cost or minimal cost. These channels developed agile, scalable ways of learning.

Making MOOCs formally introduced in the learning model could help the overall knowledge in the organization. It is the right time to do it, if not late.

Concept 6: Standard Deviation

Diversity is the beauty and strength of an organization which is in the form of gender, education, and even performance. But understanding the variation is the game-changer. Knowing the standard deviation in a particular parameter can change the rule of the game. Reward, recognition can be appropriately implemented when we only understand this concept very well as recognising the best and rewarding the best turns out to shift the performance curve upward.

Application: Performance Appraisal Giving a single, annual review means that managers and employees only get one chance for real improvement per year. It's much more effective to allow people to adjust whenever needed rather than informing them in April that, one year before, they did something wrong. In Short: Appraise continually, use AI in the process.

When closing is over, set performance parameters immediately (easy to set and based on balance sheet figures).

Evaluate all the employees based on it (with a performance data-based approach without involvement of perceptual faculty). And simply give a pop-up message (like best employee, star, or something motivational) whenever that employee is being searched on your people management software or your core banking software. This will create specific vibrations in the organization. This is what you need precisely in the public sector for aspiration building. Continue this every quarter afterwards.

Concept 7: Tribes and Silos

Though there are many aspects of the transformation journey, the most important one is reshaping the culture that exists. One of the cultural toxicity, in my view, is the SILO Effect. The Silos created inside the organization is killing the 3 Ps -People Process and Product. You can find lots of them in a division, in a solitary campus too. Cross communication is difficult, and the implementation of change is much more difficult. So breaking these SILOs should be the first transformation. This can be done by restructuring the workforce and divisions by allowing cross-flow of employees and responsibility from one to the other. And also by implementing projects by giving responsibility to all of them together. Organizations can break down silos by reexamining classification systems and job boundaries. Like HR, IT, and Data Analytics are the three main components of any sustainable policy formation. If they form their SILOs, imagine the fate.

Application: Instead of holding one-way information sessions, we should set up cross-silo deliberations that help staffs perceive the world through the eyes of customers or colleagues in other parts of the corporation. The goal is to get everybody to share information and work on creating that different input into new solutions. This happens best in face-to-face meetings that are carefully structured to allow people time to listen to one another's thinking.

Conclusion:

Strategy and innovation has a fragile line of difference. Every strategy needs innovation, and every innovation needs strategy. Hence bringing innovation into the workplace, we need to bring strategical thinking into it. Design thinking is a very dynamic approach to this problem. If we develop design thinkers across our organization, we can make innovations flourish. To be sure, it requires tools that can help identify surprising, creative breaks from conventional thinking. But it also requires tools for analyzing the competitive landscape, the dynamics threatening that landscape, and bank's resources and competencies.

We often refuse to accept an idea merely because the tone of voice in which it has been expressed is unsympathetic to us.

Friedrich Nietzsche

Instant Messaging at Work: An Overview

Digital age has many tools. Replacing the letterbox is one of the most significant activities of digitalization. Remember the days when you wait for the postal department to be guided, then came the age of mails and now the age of messages (Instant messages). At this juncture, we have many of these tools, starting from WhatsApp, Facebook messenger, telegram, and so on.

The benefits of this technology have quickly become apparent. Even in the early 2000s, scholars noted how instant messaging helped to decrease unnecessary, back-and-forth phone calls and lessen miscommunications. And **IM routs email** by offering immediate and more precise resolution to business concerns that may have remained unnoticed in inboxes.

In our bank, the use of WhatsApp is widespread, which is used to send instant communications to anybody in the group. It is time to explore the best practices of instant messaging at work. The most crucial problem is these structures can create communication silos, where teams who are highly integrated in one tool are unable to collaborate with departments rooted in another tool, or many a silos are

161

created within a single tool/platform(WhatsApp has limitations in some users in a group). Also ease of communication breeds distraction and informality, where instant messaging becomes a natural conduit to share non-work-related information, including details, sometimes inappropriate, of workers' personal lives.

Having said the benefits that we can reap from IM applications, we need to follow the suggested practices for better workplace management.

1) **Adopt the IMs your employees are already using:** Using IM in a diversified workplace usually depends upon the employees. For example, we, in PSB, prefer WhatsApp as a popular messaging media. But the application has its demerits.

2) **Look for any other IM tool, notably which is encrypted, and which can solve our needs.:** Apart from WhatsApp, few applications have features that can address our issues. Such IM applications can be Telegram and Slack. Let us analyze those applications.

Telegram: Telegram is a messaging application with a focus on speed and security and is super-fast, free and

162

straightforward. One can use Telegram on all her devices **at the same time**, and her messages sync seamlessly across any number of your tablets, phones, or computers. With Telegram, one can send messages, videos, photos and files of any type (doc,mp3, etc.), and create groups for up to **2L** people or **channels** for broadcasting to **unrestricted** audiences. One can write to one"s phone contacts and find people by their usernames. As a result, Telegram is like email and SMS combined and can take care of all business or personal messaging needs. In addition to this, it has provisions of **end-to-end encrypted voice calls**. Since Telegram groups can have up to **200,000 members**, it support **hashtags, replies, and mentions** that help keep order and keep communication in large groups **efficient**. **Admins can be appointed with advanced tools** to help these communities prosper in peace. Anyone can join **public groups**, and these are powerful platforms for debates and collecting feedback. Apart from these features, the messages can be sent with self-destructing instructions.

USE: This application can board all one lac employees in it, which means we can use it as a tool for reaching out to all employees. This groups can be used as a tool for coaching and training through various channels through it. The model can be used in the Mission Parivartan division to implement Design thinking and can act as a tool of change management.

Slack: Work in Slack happens in channels – a single place to communicate, share files, and make decisions. Channels bring together cross-functional and cross-departmental teams, so everyone always stays on the same page. The conversations become common institutional knowledge. Working in Slack provides faster access to people and information, reducing the number of meetings and emails it takes to get work done. Organized channels and powerful search put instant communication and knowledge at everyone's fingertips. Collaborate from anywhere with the fast, secure, and fully-featured mobile app. With on-the-go access to direct and group messaging, file sharing, calls, and tools, you can move seamlessly from desktop to mobile and back again. When opted for enterprise mode (Paid), it supports large scale collaboration and alignment with support for up to 500,000 users, streamlined administration with centralized controls and customizable policies, Peace of mind with enterprise-grade security and compliance, including enterprise key management and HIPAA support.

USE: The same as Instagram with additional support when we use an enterprise model.

3) **Set rules for the use of IM applications.** The most critical aspect of IM applications is the excessive use in the form of trash messages. Strict laws need to be placed before launching any platform.

4) **Promote face to face interaction:** The IM applications will reduce the need of face to face communication. So, we must take the utmost care to promote face to face interaction.

If we follow these protocols, any IM platform will remain a beneficial workplace tool rather than a nuisance. We need to customize our requirements and choose the desired platform suited for the best needs of corporations.

ॐ सह नाववतु ।

सह नौ भुनक्तु ।

सह वीर्यं करवावहै ।

तेजस्वि नावधीतमस्तु मा विद्विषावहै ।

ॐ शान्तिः शान्तिः शान्तिः ॥

Shanti Mantra

Defining Enterprise 2.0

As we have discussed earlier digital communication will improve our efficiency to a great extent. Further, we can improve by utilizing Enterprise 2.0 in communicating with employees.

Enterprise 2.0 is the corporate integration of online social networking and collaborative technologies into a company's business processes. The purpose of Enterprise 2.0 is to flatten and democratize a company's communications with its customers, partners and employees.

Andrew McAfee of the HBS (Harvard Business School) who coined the term advocates the three attributes to judge if a specific use of technology qualifies as an Enterprise 2. 0. The criteria are; Freeform, Frictionless and emergent.

Freeform: people come together as equals within the environment created by technology, and do pretty much whatever they want.

Frictionless: Ease of participation and contribution.

Emergent: the appearance over time within a system of higher-level patterns or structures arising from large numbers of unplanned and undirected low-level interactions.

167

This enterprise 2.0 will be effectively useful in managing innovation and engaging employees. Ee discussed earlier in this book about Design Thinking and making of an organization as an organization of counsellors. Enterprise 2.0 will take us to the goal.

This will lead to a decline in HPPO(Highest Paid Persons Opinion) and truly democratize the innovation landscape.

It will be imperative to quote interaction of McAfee with MIT Sloan Management Review

"The central change with Enterprise 2.0 and ideas of managing knowledge [is] not managing knowledge anymore — get out of the way, let people do what they want to do, and harvest the stuff that emerges from it because good stuff will emerge. So, it's been a fairly deep shift in thinking about how to capture and organize and manage knowledge in an organization."

What will be the use of the Enterprise 2.0 in PSBs? The significant benefits will be ideation, employee engagement and boost in productivity. We can do this by a single process of integration, and the employees will be allowed to interact among themselves in a social site created by the bank. The bank can pose significant concerns in the said platform. The interests are to be addressed by employees irrespective of their rank.

168

Participation of senior officials are very crucial step for the success. The moderators of the platform or the divisional heads of the question raised will be monitoring the conversations and take away all the thing they needed.

If we can make the Enterprise 2.0, freeform, frictionless and emergent, we will reap the benefits years to come.

ॐ दयौः शान्तिरन्तरिक्षं शान्तिः

पृथिवी शान्तिरापः शान्तिरोषधयः शान्तिः ।

वनस्पतयः शान्तिर्विश्वेदेवाः शान्तिर्ब्रह्म शान्तिः

सर्वं शान्तिः शान्तिरेव शान्तिः सा मा शान्तिरेधि ॥

ॐ शान्तिः शान्तिः शान्तिः ॥

Shanti Mantra

169

Chapter 4: Conclusion

Business units are supposed to face disruptions by one or other means. The recent reason is Covid-19. This crisis forced many business models to adapt to remote workforce suddenly. Moreover, many burning issues like mental health, joy, freelancing, work-life balance or cost structure might have forced corporations to adopt work from home principles.

Now, when we face the changes suddenly, we have to deal with many uncertainties. Centralized offices are in an advantageous position in solving problems, but work from home is otherwise. Moreover, the workflow is not known to the bank exhaustively as till now; we did not require pulverizing the work. Apart from it, the monitoring system of work is not appropriate for remote working.

So, all these aspects made the situation not compatible with the changing scenario. So, what will be the solution to the said problem?

We can analyze the whole issue in fragments like – 1—the work to be performed 2. The people to be chosen 3. The culture to be created 4. The work to be monitored

1. The task: Banking business is too complex to be digital and remote-friendly. Banking thrives on one-one customer interaction, and cyber risk and other related matters force this business to perform in a centralized environment. But is this all about? There is at least some possibility to reimagine the task. If we want to develop a work from home framework for banks, first of all, we need to understand the whole working process. The process includes the types of work, the nature of work, the volume of work. Then, we need to know the approximate time taken to

complete a particular task in different environmental conditions and different efficiency conditions. Once we achieve this fragmentation, we will be in a position to evaluate all the work and differentiate the work which can be done from home, or office. We can use compliance of regulations to find the framework of operation. In short, we need to implement the fundamentals of IDENTINOMICS into solving the critical issue.

2. The People: While talking about change, it is the people that matters first. Choosing the right people for the proper work is the key. In an organization, we will find three broad categories of people; Self-motivated, neutral and negatively motivated. The first two categories of people are essential for an organization to thrive. To distinguish these people, we need to apply IDENTINOMICS and digitalization processes into the system. The principles of KYE will play a significant role in this. Once, we follow the system and identify the category of people; we may employ them accordingly. Quantification of work and performance can give rise to continuous evaluation of the employees. Those staff opt for work from home task has to put forth their return to a proper standard and continuously evaluated.

3. The Culture: All said and done, the cultural landscape of a company matters the most in remote-working environment. This culture leads to the path of success if it is a nurturing one and leads to chaos if it is toxic. The nurturing culture is developed by employee engagement, coaching, peer coaching. While there are incredible benefits to work remotely, there are also challenges, particularly for those employees who rely on the routine and social atmosphere of an office or work site. Peer

172

coaching comes into play in these scenarios. Coaching from seniors in handholding and coping with the changing nature of the job will be a more significant boost for employee morale. Managers, when they observe time signal correctly about their remote employees, they will empathetically and effectively connect with the employees. These small changes in culture with the utilization of soft skills and digitalization could help us effectively building a remote work culture.

4. Monitoring the work: Remote work, once a rare and innovative strategy used by tech companies, is no longer an outlier business practice. Decentralized teams face several challenges. These can have damaging consequences if not appropriately addressed, but they can be overcome. One of the critical features is monitoring the work. We are stressing so much on compliance due to this reason. Compliance features once developed, must be meticulously followed, and with the help of IDENTINOMICS and digitalization, we will overcome the hurdles posed by the new system in place.

It is the time to use Compliance, Identinomics and Digitalization

ॐ पूर्णमदः पूर्णमिदं पूर्णात्पूर्णमुदच्यते ।

पूर्णस्य पूर्णमादाय पूर्णमेवावशिष्यते ॥

ॐ शान्तिः शान्तिः शान्तिः ‖ Shanti Mantra

effectively for transformation in the banking sector.

173

Bibliography

The future of bank risk management - McKinsey & Company.
https://www.mckinsey.com/~/media/mckinsey/business%20functions/risk/
our%20insights/the%20future%20of%20bank%20risk%20management/t
he-future-of-bank-risk-management-full-report.ashx

https://warwick.ac.uk/research/warwickcommission/financialreform/report
/chapter_1.pdf

http://yojana.gov.in/Yojana%20Jnauary%202018.pdf

NPCI. https://www.npci.org.in/product-overview/upi-product-overview

Meet 'Generation Mute' - Times of India.
https://timesofindia.indiatimes.com/life-style/health-fitness/de-
stress/meet-generation-mute/articleshow/63627597.cms

What is iBeacon? A Guide to Beacons | iBeacon.com Insider.
http://www.ibeacon.com/what-is-ibeacon-a-guide-to-beacons/

Will Augmented and Virtual Reality Replace the Bank Branch?.
https://thefinancialbrand.com/65828/ar-vr-voice-chatbot-bank-branch-
replacement-trends/

The power of habit by Charles Duhigg

Slack. https://slack.com/intl/en-au/enterprise

The Decline of the HPPO (Highest Paid Person's Opinion).
https://sloanreview.mit.edu/article/the-decline-of-the-hppo-highest-paid-
persons-opinion/

www.ingramcontent.com/pod-product-compliance
Lightning Source LLC
Chambersburg PA
CBHW071458220526
45472CB00003B/842